NOT LIKE THE GENTILES:
MARRIAGE RULES IN THE LETTERS OF PAUL

SOCIETY OF BIBLICAL LITERATURE

DISSERTATION SERIES

Charles H. Talbert, Editor

Number 80

NOT LIKE THE GENTILES: MARRIAGE RULES
IN THE LETTERS OF PAUL

by
O. Larry Yarbrough

O. Larry Yarbrough

NOT LIKE THE GENTILES
Marriage Rules in the Letters of Paul

Scholars Press
Atlanta, Georgia

NOT LIKE THE GENTILES
MARRIAGE RULES IN THE LETTERS OF PAUL

O. Larry Yarbrough

Ph.D., 1984
Yale University

Advisor:
Wayne A. Meeks

Library of Congress Cataloging-in-Publication Data

Yarbrough, O. Larry.
  Not like the Gentiles.

  (Dissertation series / Society of Biblical
Literature ; no. 80)
  Originally presented as the author's thesis
(Ph. D.)—Yale University, 1984.
  Bibliography: p.
  1. Marriage—Biblical teaching. 2. Bible. N.T.
Thessalonians, 1st IV, 3-8—Criticism, interpretation,
etc. 3. Bible. N.T. Corinthians, 1st VII—Criticism,
interpretation, etc. 4. Marriage—History. 5. Sexual
ethics—History. I. Title. II. Series: Dissertation
series (Society of Biblical Literature) ; no. 80.

Printed in the United States of America
on acid-free paper

To Amy

Contents

Acknowledgments

It is with a deep sense of gratitude to those who have taught me that I submit this dissertation for publication. I count myself fortunate indeed to have studied with scholars such as Earl Gossett and Roy Wells of Birmingham-Southern College, Brian Beck and C.F.D. Moule of Cambridge University, L.E. Keck (then) of Emory University, and Abraham Malherbe and Wayne Meeks of Yale University. From each of them, and from those who taught me earlier in my life, I have learned much and am grateful. To enter now into the guild of scholar-teachers to which they belong is an honor.

My special thanks go to Professor Wayne Meeks who not only directed the dissertation but early in my graduate studies helped me shape the kinds of questions which gave rise to it. And as every scholar knows, to learn to ask the right questions is the most important lesson for productive research.

I am grateful to the Episcopal Divinity School of Cambridge, Massachusetts for allowing me to use its excellent library facilities while living in the Boston area. The entire staff of the library was most helpful. I also wish to thank Professor J. Paul Sampley of the Boston University School of Theology for being willing to discuss various parts of this work and for his encouragement in the process of writing it. And I thank the members of the Boston University New Testament colloquium for allowing me to participate in its meetings and for expressing interest in the work of a sojourner among them.

For financial support during my research I gratefully acknowledge the Dempster Graduate Fellowships awarded by the Board of Higher Education and Ministry of the United Methodist Church. For underwriting the cost of preparing the manuscript for publication, I thank Middlebury College.

To my wife Amy I express my deepest thanks.

Middlebury, Vermont
January, 1985

Note on
Abbreviations and References

Abbreviations used in this work are those recommended by the Society of Biblical Literature. They are listed in the 1980 edition of the *Member's Handbook*, pp 83-97.

References in footnotes are identified by the author's name and the date of publication. The reader will find complete information on each reference in the Bibliography.

Introduction

In his *Second Apology* Justin Martyr tells of a woman who, having come to the knowledge of the teachings of Christ, rejected her former life of intemperance and encouraged her husband to do the same. When he refused, she divorced him, "considering it wicked to live any longer as a wife with a husband who sought in every way means of indulging in pleasure contrary to the law of nature, and in violation of what is right."[1] Because he did not agree to the divorce, however, the woman's husband brought charges against her, among which was the accusation that she was a Christian. She appealed to the emperor (Antoninus Pius) and, Justin notes with satisfaction, was acquitted.[2]

In a much more vivid way the *Acts of Paul and Thecla* recounts a similar story.[3] Thecla, the heroine of this apocryphal work, was betrothed to a man named Thamyris. When she heard Paul proclaim the word of God "concerning continence and the resurrection," however, she renounced her engagement, declaring that as a follower of Paul she would remain a virgin. Both Thamyris and Thecla's own mother sought to dissuade her from such a course. When their entreaties fell on deaf ears, they vilified her and brought her to trial before the local magistrates, who sentenced her to death. It was only through God's intervention that she escaped this fate, fulfilled her vow, and joined in the Pauline mission.

These two stories dramatically illustrate the difficulties which could

---

[1] *Second Apology* 2. Trans. Roberts and Donaldson 1913, 188. Text in Goodspeed 1914.

[2] Not to be outdone, her husband then turned against her teacher in the faith, of whom the officials were less tolerant—they led him away to be punished.

[3] Text in Lipsius 1891. Eng. trans. in Hennecke-Schneemelcher 1965.

beset a marriage when one of the partners became a believer and rejected
his or her former way of life. How frequently did such difficulties arise
for early Christians? It is difficult to say.[4] But interestingly enough, the
question of remaining married to an unbeliever was already raised during
the early days of the Pauline mission.[5]

That the question of remaining married to an unbeliever arose among
the followers of Paul should not really be surprising, however, for Paul
himself declared that if any one is in Christ the old order has passed away
and all things have been made new.[6] Indeed, he wrote to the Corinthians
that they should no longer associate with immoral people.[7] Could this not
be interpreted to mean that believers should separate themselves from
the unbelieving partners? It could, and among Paul's followers in Corinth
apparently was.

The emergence of the question regarding whether believers should
separate themselves from their unbelieving partners raises other questions
for us. What *did* Paul say about marriage? And, equally important, what
was the significance of what he said for the day-to-day life of his followers? That is, how did becoming a believer affect one's decisions regarding
marriage? Did the passing of the old order involve the complete denial of
marriage? After all, marriage was one of the fundamental institutions of
that order, so that rejecting it would be a means of demonstrating separation from the old and participation in the new. If complete denial of
marriage were not called for, did becoming a believer mean that one
should marry only within the fellowship of believers? If this were the
case, the consequences could be great, for the choice of a spouse would be
greatly limited, especially if the community itself were small. And if one

---

[4]A number of references do occur to such difficulties in early Christian
literature. See, in addition to these two examples, *Recognitions of
Clement* 2:29; Tertullian *Apology* 3; and Eusebius *On the Theophany* 4:12.
I hope to explore this question in a later examination of marriage in early
Christianity.

[5]1 Cor 7:12-16.

[6]2 Cor 5:17.

[7]In a letter to which Paul refers in 1 Cor 5:9. If 2 Cor 6:14-7:1 was
written by Paul, it too would lead one to ask about remaining married to
an unbeliever. There are so many problems related to this passage, however, that I have chosen not to include it among the texts treated in this
study. Although its origin is still debated, the general consensus is that
2 Cor 6:14-7:1 is a "slightly Christianized piece of Qumran theology"
(Dahl 1977, 63).

were allowed to marry only in the community of believers, were there
other criteria which obtained in the selection of a spouse? If so, were
these criteria different from those employed by the surrounding world?
Finally, if one were allowed to marry, and if, as Paul claimed, the end of
the world were at hand, what about having children? Would they be members of the community also? How should they be raised and educated?

Of course I am not the first to ask such questions, for the very Corinthians who inquired concerning separation from unbelieving partners
raised many of these questions as well.[8] Nor is mine the first attempt to
examine the ways Paul addresses them. In this century there have been
three major studies of Paul's treatment of marriage: Herbert Preisker's
Christeneum und Ehe in den ersten drei Jahrhunderten; Gerhard Delling's
Paulus' Stellung zu Frau und Ehe; and Heinrich Baltensweiler's *Die Ehe im
Neuen Testament.*[9]

This study differs from these earlier ones in several ways. As one might
expect, it differs in matters of exegetical detail. In fact, of the three
works, Baltensweiler's is the only one given to a close reading of the text,
the other two being concerned with the questions of the history of reli-
gions school. More importantly, however, this study differs from the
others in its approach, for while I share Preisker's and Delling's interest in
the discussion of marriage in Jewish and Greco-Roman literature, I am
concerned with discovering the significance of Paul's treatment of marriage and sexual morality—both for himself and for his followers—and not
simply with determining what he actually said. Thus, when I ask why does
Paul speak of marriage as he does? I have something quite different in
mind than Preisker and Delling. The difference may be seen most acutely
in comparison with Delling's work. For although he attributes Paul's
negative view of marriage to his Jewish roots (erroneously, I think) and to
his Christ-mysticism,[10] he cannot avoid the attempt to discover a psychological motivation at work prior to these reasons. In the first instance, I
am not convinced that Paul's view of marriage (and women) was as negative as Delling claims.[11] But even if it is, there is no evidence for his

[8]Assuming that Paul's discussion of marriage in 1 Corinthians 7 deals
with a number of questions that were addressed to him by the Corinthian
community. See below, chapter 4.

[9]Preisker 1927; Delling 1931; Baltensweiler 1976. See also Kähler
1960; Thurian [1959] ; and von Allmen 1963. For the numerous articles on
marriage in Pauline ethics, see the bibliography.

[10]See pp 66-69 and his conclusions pp 141-152. In this regard Delling
agrees with Preisker (127-132).

assertion that Paul came to such a view because his mother died early,
leaving him to be raised in a masculine environment devoid of all feminine
presence which might have allowed him to develop some appreciation of
family life.[12]
No doubt Paul's religious experience (and his apocalyptic world-view)
contributed to his view of marriage and sexual morality. But other factors
were at work as well. And primary among these was his concern with the
life of the communities under his charge. For in every instance in which
Paul discusses marriage and sexual morality, the identity and good order
of the community is at issue. This aspect of his discussion will be the
focus of our attention here.
To be sure, Baltensweiler also asks, "What *function* does marriage serve
in the life of men and of society?"[13] But he asks the question from a
theological perspective and not with a view to how Paul's treatment of
marriage functioned within the life of the communities he founded.
Indeed, when he examines the relevant texts, the question of their function never arises in any notable way. By addressing the question of the
function of Paul's treatment of marriage and sexual morality, therefore,
this study should make a significant contribution to our understanding of
Pauline ethics.[14]
In analyzing Paul's treatment of marriage and sexual morality we will
be concerned with two passages: 1 Thess 4:3-8 and 1 Corinthians 7.[15]
Whether 1 Thess 4:3-8 in fact deals with marriage is of course a matter of
debate in scholarly circles. Thus, when we turn to it, one of our first tasks
will be to support the claim that it does. Having done so, we must then
ask how and why Paul treats it as he does. Next, we will take up the
discussion in 1 Corinthians 7. No attempt will be made to resolve all the
problems in this difficult chapter, but again, by addressing the question of

---

[11]See below, chapter 5.

[12]See p. 144.

[13]1976, 11. My trans., Baltensweiler's emphasis.

[14]On the importance of inquiring into the *function* of the beliefs and
practices of early Christian groups, see Meeks 1975, 1, 4-5, a program-
matic essay describing the approach adopted by the SBL's working group
on the social world of early Christianity. This study is to be seen as a contribution to the growing body of literature shaped by this "reformist"
approach.

[15]Colossians and Ephesians, together with their "household codes,"
most likely belong to the second generation of Pauline Christianity. I will
withhold treatment of them to a later time.

how Paul's treatment of marriage affected the community to which he was writing, we will make significant progress in understanding it.

Because we are concerned here with the significance of Paul's treatment of marriage and sexual morality and because in his discussion of these issues Paul repeatedly refers to "outsiders," it is necessary to begin this study with surveys of what these outsiders were saying about marriage and sexual morality. This will enable us to focus more clearly on what may have been distinctive about Paul's discussion. We will discover, however, that in fact there was very little that was distinctive. But this in itself is an important discovery, for it allows us to establish the points of contact between the Pauline mission and the larger world of Greco-Roman society (of which Judaism was a part) and thereby determine more precisely how the nature of Pauline ethics as it relates to marriage and sexual morality may have affected his followers who, after all, continued to live in a world dominated by Greco-Roman culture.

1

The Treatment of Marriage and Sexual Morality in Jewish Moral Traditions

Paul advised the Thessalonians, "Let each man know how to obtain his own wife in holiness and honor, not in the passion of desire as the Gentiles who do not know God" (1 Thess 4:4).[1] The last phrase in the formulation of this precept illustrates why any treatment of Paul's moral teaching must take Jewish traditions into account. In the first instance, "the Gentiles who do not know God" (τὰ ἔθνη τὰ μὴ εἰδότα τὸν θεὸν) belongs to the language of the Hebrew Bible, where it draws attention to the distinction between Israel and all the other nations of the world.[2] Even more telling for our purposes now, however, is Paul's reference to the Gentiles' "passion of desire," for in Jewish moral traditions, especially those of the diaspora, this is one of the primary aspects of Gentile life to which reference is made when the distinction between Israel and the nations is at issue. That is, the characterization of Gentile life as "immoral" allows Jewish writers to claim that because of their moral superiority Jews are distinct from the nations of the world.[3]

Does Paul's reference to the Gentiles' "passion of desire" serve to distinguish "believers" from "the nations" also? I suggest that it does, in part at least. But before we take up the formulation and function of Paul's

---

[1] I will give evidence for this translation in chapter 3 below.

[2] "The Gentiles" (גוים, τα ἔθνη) is used throughout the Bible in opposition to "the people of God" (עם, λαός). See the discussion in Bertram 1964, 264-269. "The Gentiles who do not know God" has an almost exact parallel in the LXX version of Jer 10:25: "The Gentiles who do not know you" (ἔθνη τὰ μὴ εἰδότα σε).

[3] As we shall see, Hellenistic writers also refer to the "passion" of foreigners, thereby claiming moral superiority for themselves. It would appear from Paul's characterization of Gentiles as those "who do not know God," however, that he is following Jewish traditions here. See below, chapter 3.

8 Not like the Gentiles

precepts in 1 Thessalonians 4 (and his adaptation of them in 1 Corinthains 7) we must examine further the treatment of marriage and sexual morality in the Jewish moral traditions. Because I am interested in discovering clues which will help in determining the function of Paul's discussion of these issues, however, I must emphasize that in examining the Jewish traditions I am not looking for verbal parallels only. For as important as verbal parallels are for analyzing the background of Paul's thought, by themselves they tell us little. I suggest therefore that we will in fact gain most from a survey of the treatment of marriage and sexual morality in the Jewish moral traditions by inquiring not only into what was said but also into why it was said. In asking this question one of the discoveries we will make is that, as suggested above, the treatment of marriage and sexual morality was one means of distinguishing Jews and Gentiles—both in the apocrypha and pseudepigrapha and in the rabbinic literature. We will also discover, however, that while this is a primary feature of the former, in the latter the treatment of marriage and sexual morality is part of a larger system, a system that defines the Jewish community not only by distinguishing it from the outside world but also by ordering every aspect of its day-to-day life.

THE MORAL TRADITIONS OF THE APOCRYPHA AND PSEUDEPIGRAPHA [4]

The claim that Jewish moral values are superior to those of the surrounding world is a common feature of the apocrypha and pseudepigrapha. It is most clearly seen in the Letter of Aristeas. Explaining why Jews abstain from eating the flesh of certain animals, the author of the Letter

---

[4]Most of the works treated in this section have their origin in the diaspora: Wisdom of Solomon, Tobit, the Letter of Aristeas, the Sibylline Oracles, *Joseph and Asenath,* the *Testament of Job, Pseudo-Phocylides,* and the writings of Philo and Josephus. Jubilees derives from Palestine and has affinities with the literature of the Essene community at Qumran, though scholars debate the precise nature of the relationship. See VanderKam 1977. Scholarly opinion is also divided over the *Testaments of the Twelve Patriarchs.* There seems to be an emerging consensus, however, that it contains many early Jewish traditions. The debate centers over when and to what extent these traditions were reworked by a Christian editor. The discovery of portions of the *Testament of Levi* among the scrolls hidden by the Essene community at the Dead Sea supports the claim that the early traditions are Palestinian in provenance. For surveys of recent literature on the *Testaments,* see Becker 1970, 129-158 and de Jonge 1975, 183-192.

states, "The division of the hoof and the separation of the claws are
intended to teach us that we must discriminate between individual actions
with a view to the practice of virtue."[5] Virtue (ἀρετή), of course, was a
concept borrowed from the Hellenistic moral tradition.[6] Nevertheless, the
Letter of Aristeas claims that for Jews the "standard of righteousness" by
which virtue it is measured is especially rigorous, since they "have been
distinctly separated from the rest of mankind."[7] As an illustration of this
higher moral standard, the Letter compares the sexual practices of Jews
with those of the nations:

> For most men defile themselves by promiscuous intercourse,
> thereby working great iniquity, and whole countries and cities
> pride themselves upon such vices. For they not only have
> intercourse with men, but they defile their own mothers and
> even their daughters. But we have been kept separate from
> such sins.[8]

The accusation that the nations practice incest first appears in Leviticus
18. After charging the people of Israel, "You shall not do as they do in the
land of Egypt, where you dwelt, and you shall not do as they do in the
Land of Canaan, to which I am bringing you," the Levitical legislators
declare in the name of Yahweh, "None of you shall approach any one near
of kin to him to uncover nakedness" (vv 2 and 6). Those near of kin include
father, mother, father's wife, sister, granddaughter, cousin, niece, etc.

In *Spec. Laws* 3.22-25, Philo takes up the question of incest with one's
sister, comparing the Jewish law with the corresponding laws of the
Athenians, Lacedaemonians, and Egyptians. He notes that while the
Athenians permit marriage with the half-sister on the father's side, and
prohibit marriage with a half-sister on the mother's side, the Lacedaemonians rule exactly the opposite. The Egyptians, he charges, "give full
liberty to marry sisters of every degree." In contrast to these, Philo states
that the law of Moses rejects all such marriages, claiming they were
regarded "with abhorrence, as alien and hostile to a commonwealth free

---

[5]*Ep. Arist.* 150. Trans. Andrews, in Charles 1913.
[6]The *topos on Virtue* (περὶ ἀρετῆς) appears throughout the literature
of the Greco-Roman moral tradition. For an overview of the "common
ethic" of Jews and Gentiles, see Collins 1983, chapter 4 and the literature
cited there.
[7]*Ep. Arist.* 151.
[8]*Ep. Arist.* 152.

from reproach and as encouragements and incitements to the vilest customs."

The other distinctive element referred to by the Letter of Aristeas is the abhorrence of intercourse with men. An exhaustive treatment of this theme in Jewish moral literature is beyond the scope of this essay.[9] But one other example may be cited to illustrate how sharp the accusations could be when the claim to moral superiority was being made:

But [the Jews] raise heavenwards holy hands, rising early from their bed and ever cleansing their flesh with water, and they honour Him alone who reigns forever, the Eternal, and after him their parents; and more than any men they are mindful of the purity of marriage. Nor do they hold unholy intercourse with boys, as do the Phoenicians, Egyptians, and Latins and spacious Hellas and many nations of other men, Persians and Galatians and all Asia, transgressing the holy law of the immortal God.[10]

The Oracle implies here that sexual immorality is the result of idolatry. This relation is made explicit in 5.386-433, where in contrast to the Jews who have "hymned forth the glory of God" and therefore abstained from "adulteries and unnatural passion for boys," idolaters have indulged in homosexual acts, prostitution and incest.

The Wisdom of Solomon also relates idolatry and immorality.[11] Especially important for our purpose is 14:26, where the charge is made that idolaters "no longer keep either their lives or their marriages pure, but either treacherously kill one another, or grieve one another by adultery." The implication, of course, is that those who worship the true God keep their marriages pure by abstaining from adulterous relations, a claim that is explicitly made in the passage from the Sibylline Books just cited. Philo makes a similar point, though without reference to idolatry, when he states that while men of other nations visit prostitutes from the age of fourteen, Jews do not do so at all.[12]

---

[9]See the recent treatments by Boswell 1980, 91-117 and Scroggs 1983, 66-98.
[10]Sib. Or. 3:591-599. Trans. Lanchester, in Charles 1913. See also 5:162.
[11]See 14:12, "The making of idols was the beginning of fornication." Compare, T. Sim. 5:3, "[fornication] is the mother of all evils ... separating from God and bringing near to Beliar." Trans. Charles 1913.
[12]On Jos. 42-43. Loeb ed.

All the examples we have examined so far refer to a specific vice when claiming that Jews are morally superior to other peoples. In many instances, however, the claim is made without any such reference. One sees this, for example, in Jubilees 22:16, where Abraham's final blessing of Jacob includes the command, "Separate thyself from the nations . . . For their works are unclean and all their ways are a pollution and an abomination and uncleanness." Later in Jubilees, Rebecca warns Jacob against taking a foreign wife, holding up before him the wives of Esau, who, being daughters of Canaan, have "embittered [her] soul with all their unclean deeds: for all their deeds are fornication and lust, there is no righteousness in them" (25:1). In passages such as these, it is presupposed that the readers to whom they are addressed will know what "fornication and lust" means, so that the accusation itself is sufficient.

When one turns from the claims that Jews are distinct from the nations because they do not practice incest and homosexual acts and the general accusation that the ways of the Gentiles are a pollution and an abomination and uncleanness to ask how the Jews are more mindful than other men of the purity of marriage (to use the language of the Sibylline Books again), one finds few indications other than the assertion that they abstain from adultery. The closest one comes to an answer to this question is the claim that Jews engage in sexual intercourse only for the procreation of children. Josephus writes in his apology *Against Apion* that this view of sexual intercourse is based on the Law of Moses: "The law requires no sexual connexions, except the natural union of man and wife, and that only for the procreation of children."[13] Similarly, the account of Rachel's attempts to conceive a child in *T. Issa.* 2:3 asserts that God answered her prayer because, "He knew that for the sake of children she wished to company with Jacob, and not for lust of pleasure (οὐ διὰ φιληδονία)." As we shall see, limiting sexual intercourse to the procreation of children was a common theme in the Hellenistic moral traditions also.[14] Indeed, Josephus and Philo, the two Jewish writers most concerned with this issue, doubtless borrowed it from the Greco-Roman moralists. Nevertheless, Philo can refer to it when distinguishing Jews from other peoples:

---

[13] *Ag. Ap.* 2.199. See also *J.W.* 2.161, where Josephus says that the Essenes do not have intercourse with their wives during pregnancy, "thus showing that their motive in marrying is not self-indulgence (δι' ἡδονήν)." Trans. Thackeray. Loeb ed.

[14] See below, chapter 2.

For [those who expose children] [15] are pleasure lovers when they mate with their wives, not to procreate children and perpetuate the race, but like pigs and goats in quest of the enjoyment which such intercourse gives.[16]

Taking his argument that procreation is the only legitimate purpose for sexual intercourse one step further, Philo scorns men "who in their craze for sexual intercourse behave unchastely, not with the wives of others, but with their own."[17] This sentiment is echoed in two of the admonitions in Pseudo-Phocylides:

> Do not deliver yourselves wholly unto unbridled sensuality towards your wife.
> For "eros" is not a god, but a passion destructive of all.

Outrage not your wife for shameful ways of intercourse.[18]

It is not clear what Philo and *Pseudo-Phocylides* mean by "unchaste behavior" and "shameful ways of intercourse." But one assumes that they refer to practices such as fellatio and cunnilingus, both of which may be seen depicted on Greek vases and Roman murals.[19] But again, it should be noted that warnings against engaging in sexual intercourse only for the sake of pleasure were common in Greco-Roman moral traditions and that, in fact, Philo and *Pseudo-Phocylides* owe much to these traditions.[20]

It is important to note the similarities between Jewish moral traditions regarding the purpose of sexual intercourse and those of the Hellenistic moralists not simply because they demonstrate Hellenistic Judaism's assimilation to its environment but also because noting the similarities

---

[15] In the Jewish moral traditions this was another vice characteristic of Gentiles.
[16] *Spec. Laws* 3.113. Trans. Colson. Loeb Ed. See also *On Cher.* 43, 50; *On Jos.* 43; *Pre. Stud.* 12; *On Crea.* 161; *On Abr.* 137-248; *Deca.* 119; *Moses* 29; *Who is the Heir* 164; *On Virt.* 207; *On Rewards* 108-109; *Ques. and Answ. on Gen.* 3.21; 4.86. *The Worse Attacks* 120.
[17] *Spec. Laws* 3.9. Trans. Colson. Loeb ed.
[18] *Ps. Phoc.* 193-194 and 189. Trans. van der Horst 1978.
[19] See the discussion of *Ps. Phoc.* 189 in van der Horst 1978, 239-241. Fellatio was commonly depicted in Greek and Roman art and pottery; cunnilingus much more rarely. See the discussion, with figures, in Johns 1982, chapter 6. For the erotic art in Pompeii, see Grant 1975.
[20] On Philo's debt to the Greco-Roman moral traditions, see Wendland 1895 and Heinemann 1932. The most important work on *Pseudo-Phocylides* now is van der Horst 1978.

calls attention to the polemical nature of the Jewish claims. To be sure, if one considers Hecataeus of Abdera's remark that Jews had special customs regarding burial and marriage, it appears that even among the Gentiles there was a recognition that in the practice of marriage Jews were different.[21] Indeed, it may well be that abstaining from prostitutes was an expression of this difference. Even so, however, the Jewish claims were polemical in nature. And their purpose, I suggest, was to remind Jews of the diaspora that they were different and to encourage them to remain faithful to the traditions of their fathers. This becomes clear when one examines the primary result of the claims that regarding marriage and sexual morality Jews were morally superior to the nations—they were prohibited from intermarrying with them.

The prohibition against marrying foreigners first becomes a major issue during the period after the fall of Jerusalem in 587 B.C.E. The Deuteronomic History promulgates this rule by harking back to the time of the Conquest. After listing the seven nations which were in the land of Canaan, the Historian declares in the name of Yahweh, "You shall make no covenants with them," adding more specifically, "You shall not make marriages with them."[22] In the period of the resettlement under Ezra and Nehemiah concern with this commandment is even greater, having broken it being interpreted as one of the causes for the fall of Jerusalem.[23] This leads to a reissuing of the command:

> For we have forsaken thy commandments, which thou didst command by thy servants the prophets, saying "The land which you are entering, to take possession of it, is a land unclean with the pollutions of the peoples of the land with their abominations which have filled it from end to end with their uncleanness. Therefore, give not your daughters to their sons, neither take their daughters for your sons."[24]

---

[21]Hecataeus' comment is recorded in Didorus *Hist.* 40. On the various fragments attributed to Hecataeus, see Collins 1983, 137-141. Justin accuses the Jews of practicing polygamy (*Dial.* 134, 141). But it is doubtful that this was at all common for the majority of the Jewish population. See Moore 1927, vol 2, 122; Epstein 1942, 12-25; and Safrai 1976, 748-750. CD 4.12ff explicitly bans polygamy. See also *Ps. Phoc.* 205.
[22]Deut 7:1-5. See also Ex 34:11-16, which parallels Deut 7:1-5.
[23]Ezra 9:13.
[24]Ezra 9:10b-12a.

Indeed, those who returned with Ezra and Nehemiah were made to give up the wives they had married while in exile.[25] One of the most interesting ways of examining the development of the concern with prohibiting marriage with foreigners is to trace the interpretation of Genesis 34, the account of the rape of Dinah. In Genesis 34 itself there are two issues in Shechem's attempt to marry Dinah after raping her: the fear of losing property to one of the seven nations and the disgrace (חרפה) in allowing a daughter of Israel to be married to one who is uncircumcised. In later accounts, however, only the second issue is treated and even it is reinterpreted. For example, when Josephus recounts the story of the rape of Dinah, he does not refer to Jacob's giving her to Shechem as a "disgrace" but, more pointedly, as "unlawful."[26]

Jubilees 30, however, is even more interesting, for here the deuteronomic tradition we noted earlier and a midrashic interpretation of Lev 18:21 and 20:2-5 are worked into the narrative of Genesis 34. Jubilees 30:1-6 summarizes the narrative of Genesis 34, concluding:

> And thus let it not again be done from henceforth that a daughter of Israel be defiled; for judgment is ordained in heaven against them that they should destroy with the sword all the men of the Shechemites because they had wrought shame in Israel.

Here, the "shame of Israel" is the rape of Dinah, as in Genesis 34. In v 7, however, a shift occurs. Now it is the man who gives his daughter or sister "to any man who is of the seed of the Gentiles" who has "wrought shame in Israel." Moreover, just as death was ordained in heaven against the sons of Israel for slaying the Shechemites, so too the heavenly tablets[27] decree that the man who brings shame on Israel by giving his daughter to a Gentile "shall surely die, and he shall be stoned with stones." V 10 offers the proof text for this judgment, Lev 18:21: "he has given of his seed to Moloch," the punishment for which, according to Lev 20:2-5, is death by stoning.[28] V 11 gives further sanction against giving one's daughter to a

---

[25]Ezra 10:9-44.

[26]Ἰάκωβος . . . οὔτε νόμιμον ἡγούμενος ἀλλοφύλῳ συνοικίζειν τὴν θυγατέρα. Ant. 1:338. Loeb ed.

[27]On the significance of "the heavenly tablets," see Nickelsburg 1981, 144.

[28]This interpretation of Lev 18:21 also occurs in Tg. Ps.-J. M. Meg. 4:9, however, refutes it, declaring that those who interpret "gives his seed to Moloch" this way should be "put to silence with a rebuke." Most modern

Gentile, appealing to the deuteronomic tradition: "And do thou, Moses, command the children of Israel and exhort them not to give their daughters to the Gentiles and do not take for their sons any of the daughters of the Gentiles, for this is abominable before the Lord." Finally, v 12 returns to Genesis 34, alluding to the disgrace associated with giving one's daughter to the uncircumcised:

> It is a reproach to Israel, to those who give, and to those that take the daughters of the Gentiles; for it is all unclean and abominable to Israel. And Israel will not be free from this uncleanness if it has a wife of the daughters of the Gentiles, or has given any of its daughters to a man who is of any of the Gentiles.

This account of Genesis 34 is striking for the way it interweaves so many traditions regarding the prohibition against marrying foreigners. Thus, it demonstrates that to give one's daughter to a Gentile or to take a Gentile as a wife is a disgrace, unlawful, and unclean. Moreover, the prohibition includes all Gentiles, and not simply those of the seven nations listed in Deuteronomy 7.

As one might expect, one of the most frequently cited reasons for prohibiting marriage with foreigners is the fear that foreign wives will "turn your sons from following [Yahweh], to serve other gods" (Deut 7:4). While many examples of this concern could be listed,[29] I limit discussion here to the most interesting one. Interrupting his account of the incest laws of Leviticus 18, Philo addresses the prohibition against marrying foreigners:

> But also [Moses] says, do not enter into the partnership of marriage with a member of a foreign nation, lest some day conquered by the forces of opposing custom you surrender and stray unawares from the paths that lead to piety and turn aside into a pathless wild. And though perhaps you yourself will hold your ground steadied from your earliest years by the admirable instructions instilled into you by your parents, with

---

scholars take the phrase in question as a reference to child sacrifice. See, for example, Noth 1977, 147-149. This is also the interpretation of m. Sanh. 7:7.

[29] See, for example, the warning to Solomon that his foreign wives "will turn your heart after their gods" (I Kings 11:2) and Josephus' commentary on this verse in Ant. 8.191-193. Loeb ed.

the holy laws always as their keynote, there is much to be
feared for your sons and daughters. It may well be that they,
enticed by spurious customs which they prefer to the genuine,
are likely to unlearn the honour due to the one God, and that
is the first and last stage of supreme misery.[30]

This passage is striking because it comes from one who knows well "the
forces of opposing customs" and has in fact made much use of them.
Philo's concern here is essentially practical, for his contrast of the first
generation, which is well grounded in the law and thus safeguarded from
the threat of "opposing custom," with the second generation, which is
unable to distinguish "genuine" from "spurious" custom and thus open to
the dangers of the surrounding world, reflects the fears one finds in an
immigrant population concerned with maintaining its identity in a new,
alien culture. For Philo, therefore, prohibiting intermarriage between
Jews and their Alexandrian neighbors was a way of insuring the future
integrity of the Alexandrian Jewish community, which was essential for
preserving "the honour due to the one God."

The fear that marriage with a foreigner may lead to apostasy is also
expressed as the fear of contamination through contact with the impurity
of foreigners. Such language of course stems from the priestly tradition.
Leviticus 18 describes the sexual practices of the nations of Canaan with
terms such as "wickedness" (זמה; LXX ἀσέβημα), "abomination" (תועבה,
LXX βδέλυγμα), and "perversion" (תבל, LXX μυσερόν), declaring that to
engage in them is to share in the nations' defilement and, as a result, to
suffer their fate—expulsion from the land. The relation to marriage with
foreigners is more explicit in Jubilees 22. Here, as we have seen, Abraham's final blessing includes the command, "Separate thyself from the
nations . . . For their works are unclean and all their ways are a pollution
and an abomination and uncleanness" (v 16). The blessing continues:

> May the Most High God help thee . . . and remove thee from
> the nations' uncleanness and from all their error. Be thou
> ware, my son Jacob, of taking a wife from any seed of the
> daughters of Canaan.

This passage is important not only because it refers to abstaining from
marriage with foreigners to avoid being contaminated by their uncleanness, but also because the form in which the warning is given appears

---

[30] *Spec. Laws* 3.29. Trans. Thackeray. Loeb ed.

frequently in the Jewish moral traditions. Moreover, in each case in which the warning occurs, it is given by a father to his sons. Thus, it would appear that in Jubilees 22:19-20 we have discovered a fixed formula dealing with marriage to a foreign woman.³¹ In two instances, only the prohibition itself occurs. In *Joseph and Asenath* 7:6 Joseph recalls the precept of his father, "Keep yourselves, children, securely from a strange woman so as not to have fellowship with her, for fellowship with her is ruin and destruction." (φυλάξατε τέκνα ἑαυτοὺς ἰσχυρῶς ἀπὸ γυναικὸς τοῦ μὴ κοινωνῆσαι αὐτῇ, ἀπώλεια γάρ ἐστι καὶ διαφθορά).³² And in *Testament of Job* 45:4 Job gathers his children around his death bed and exhorts his sons, "Do not take for yourselves a foreign wife" (μὴ λάβετε ἑαυτοῖς ἐκ τῶν ἀλλοτρίων).³³

In two other instances, however, the prohibition against marrying foreign women is preceded by a precept echoing Abraham's prayer that God will remove Jacob from the nations' uncleanness, though in both instances "immorality" rather than "uncleanness" is used. In Tobit 4:12 Tobit counsels his son Tobias, "Beware, my son, of all immorality. First of all take a wife from the descendants of your fathers and do not marry a foreign woman." (πρόσεχε σεαυτῷ, παιδίον, ἀπὸ πάσης πορνείας καὶ γυναῖκα πρῶτον λαβὲ ἀπὸ τοῦ σπέρματος τῶν πατέρων σου· μὴ λάβῃς γυναῖκα ἀλλοτρίαν).³⁴ And in *T. Levi* 9:9-10 Levi admonishes his children, "Beware of the spirit of fornication; for this shall continue and shall by thy seed pollute the holy place. Take, therefore, to thyself a wife without blemish or pollution, while thou art young, and not of the race of strange nations." (πρόσεχε, τέκνον, ἀπὸ τοῦ πνεύματος τῆς πορνείας· τοῦτο γὰρ ἐνδελεχιεῖ καὶ μέλλει διὰ τοῦ σπέρματός σου μιαίνειν τὰ ἅγια. λάβε οὖν σεαυτῷ γυναῖκα, ἔτι νέος ὤν, μὴ ἔχουσαν μῶμον μηδὲ βεβηλωμένην μηδὲ ἀπὸ γένους ἀλλοφύλων ἢ ἐθνῶν).³⁵

It should be abundantly clear now that the claim to moral superiority

³¹In 25:1-13, when Rebecca warns Jacob not to follow the example of Esau, he responds that he will not marry a woman from Canaan because he remembers the words of Abraham. And in 27:10 Isaac gives Jacob his blessing and warns him, "Do not take a wife of any of the daughters of Canaan." Immediately prior to this Rebecca had said to Isaac, "If Jacob take a wife from among the daughters of the land [of Canaan], for what purpose do I further live; for the daughters of Canaan are evil." Trans. Charles 1913.
³²Text from Philonenko 1968. Trans. Brooks 1918.
³³Text and trans. Kraft 1974.
³⁴Text from Rahlfs 1935. Trans. RSV.
³⁵Text from de Jonge 1978. Trans. Charles 1913.

and the resulting prohibition against intermarriage with foreigners were
key elements in the Jewish moral traditions of the diaspora. Both the
claim and the prohibition appear throughout the traditions. Moreover, the
prohibition even assumes a fairly fixed formulation. And again, I suggest
that the purpose of these warnings was to define the Jewish community of
the diaspora more clearly and to encourage those who were members of it
to remain faithful to the community by preserving its distinct identity. I
suggest further that recognizing the importance of these elements of the
Jewish moral traditions will aid in our understanding of Paul because his
formulation of the precepts in 1 Thess 4:3b-4 is strikingly similar to the
precepts we have noted in Jubilees 22, Tob 4:12, and *T. Levi* 9:9-10, which
suggests that Paul himself may well use these precepts to distinguish the
community of believers and encourage them to remain faithful to their
new calling.[36]
   So far we have limited our discussion of the treatment of marriage and
sexual morality to the Jewish moral traditions of the apocrypha and
pseudepigrapha. We turn now to those of the rabbinic literature. Here we
find that while the same concerns do appear, their focus is sometimes
different. Moreover, several other concerns emerge as well. To be sure,
some of the material we will discuss now is much later than Paul. Nevertheless, these late traditions demonstrate that the issues addressed by
sectarian Judaism were also important in what was to become the main
body of Jewish thought.

THE MORAL TRADITIONS OF THE RABBINIC LITERATURE

   Like the traditions of the apocrypha and pseudepigrapha, the rabbis
distinguish between Jews and Gentiles by accusing the latter of sexual
immorality. Here too the Gentiles' immorality is attributed to their
worship of idols. And again one of the specific accusations concerns the
practice of incest. Both of these issues are found in the series of riddles
contained in *b. Yebam.* 97b.[37] For example,

> [Who can say:] "He whom I carry on my shoulder is my brother
> and my son and I am his sister?" This is possible when an
> idolater cohabited with his daughter.

---

[36]I will examine these similarities further in chapter 3.
[37]All translations from the Mishnah are from Danby 1933. Translations
from the Babylonian Talmud are from the Epstein edition (1935-1948).

[Who can say:] "Greetings to you my son; I am the daughter of
your sister?" This is possible where an idolater cohabited with
his daughter's daughter.

The claim that Gentiles are immoral may also be seen in such passages
as *m. ʿAbod. Zar.* 2:1. Although this mishnah deals primarily with the
dangers of staying at inns (which were renowned in antiquity for their
immoral character[38]), it also speaks of the Gentiles' sexual promiscuity.

Cattle may not be left in the inns of the Gentiles since they
    are suspected of bestiality;
nor may a woman remain alone with them since they are
    suspected of lewdness (הערות);
nor may a man remain alone with them since they are sus-
    pected of shedding blood.

The characterization of homosexual acts as peculiarly representative
of Gentile immorality is much rarer in the rabbinic literature than in the
sectarian traditions, especially in the early period. The clearest example
of this view of Gentiles in rabbinic literature is *Sipra Lev.* 18:3, where
homosexual marriages (both male and female) are listed among the vices
practiced by Egyptians and Canaanites. It is implied, however, in the
warning that one should not send one's sons to a Gentile to study, learn a
trade, or be alone with him in any circumstances.[39] More explicit accusations come from the later period. *Gen. Rab.* 63:10, for example, referring
to Rome, laments: "Must we not only serve other nations but this one as
well, who is immorally abused, like women?"[40]

The prohibition against marrying foreigners because of their immorality was a frequent theme in rabbinic literature. And again, many of the
discussions focus on the interpretation of Deut 7:1-5. This passage is
central in a ruling attributed to the Schools of Hillel and Shammai:

The Biblical ordinance [against intermarriage] is restricted to
the seven nations and does not include other heathen peoples;
and [the schools of Hillel and Shammai] came and decreed
against these also.[41]

---

[38]See Malherbe 1977, 65-66 and the literature cited there.
[39]*T. ʿAbod. Zar.* 10:2.
[40]Trans. Freedman, in Freedman-Simon 1939.
[41]*B. ʿAbod. Zar.* 36b. According to *m. Nid.* 4:3, however, the Schools
debate whether the blood of Gentile women is unclean—the Shammaites

According to R. Simeon b. Yoḥai the reason for this ruling is to be found in Deut 7:4a, since, he argues, this includes "all women who would turn [their husbands aside from the worship of God]." This interpretation accords with the concern with idolatry we observed in the apocrypha and pseudepigrapha. R. Naḥman b. Isaac, however, offers another reason. He states that the Schools of Hillel and Shammai ruled that the Biblical ordinance applied to all nations because "their daughters should be considered as in the state of *niddah* [the period of menstruation, which renders a woman unclean] from their cradle."[42]

From 70 C.E. onward yet another reason for avoiding marriage with foreigners appears: concern with the children of mixed marriages. Unlike Philo, however, the concern is not with the apostasy of these children, but with their status as Jews. *B. Qidd.* 68b is illustrative. The issue debated here is how one knows that a child takes the status of its mother. Gen 21:4 is cited as proof that the child of a Canaanite bondswoman takes the mother's status as an outsider. The question is then raised concerning the child of a freeborn Gentile woman and an Israelite. In answer to this question R. Yoḥanan gives a fuller version of the saying attributed to R. Simeon b. Yoḥai just cited:

> Because Scripture saith, "For he will turn away thy son from following me:" thy son by an Israelite woman is called "thy son," but thy son from a heathen is not "thy son" but "her son." Now that [verse] refers to the seven nations! Whence do we know it of other nations? Scripture saith, "For he will turn away [thy son]," which includes all who turn [him] away.

Like the traditions we examined earlier, therefore, the rabbis distinguish Jews from Gentiles on the basis of their sexual morality and prohibit marriage with Gentiles. One also finds in rabbinic literature concern with limiting sexual intercourse to the procreation of children. R. Ḥuna, for example, claims that "any cohabitation which results in no increase is nothing but meretricious intercourse (בעילת זנות)."[43] *M. Yebam* 8:5 reflects a similar view, prohibiting sexual intercourse between a eunuch and his childless brother's widow or between a sterile widow and her

---

declaring that it is clean, the Hillelites that it is "like to her spittle or her urine."

[42] On the importance of the debate over *niddah*, see below.

[43] *B. Yebam* 61b. He cites Hos 4:10 as a proof text.

childless husband's brother. It is probable that sexual relations between such persons is to be regarded as fornication precisely because they are incapable of procreation.

The rabbis did not speak with one voice in this matter, however, for the Sages rejected R. Yoḥanan b. Dahabai's claim that birth defects were caused by "unnatural intercourse." They countered that "a man may do whatever he pleases with his wife," since

> Meat which comes from the abbatoir may be eaten salted, roasted, cooked, or seethed, so with fish from the fish-monger.[44]

B. Sahn. 58b echoes this debate:

> R. Eleazar said in R. Hanina's name: If a heathen had an unnatural (שלא כדרכה) connection with his wife he incurs guilt; for it is written "and he shall cleave" [Gen 2:24], which excludes unnatural intercourse. Raba objected: Is there anything for which a Jew is not punishable and a heathen is?

The implication of Raba's objection is that "unnatural intercourse" is not prohibited to a Jew, which means that in his view procreation was not the only reason for engaging in sexual intercourse.

Nonetheless, the rabbis were unanimous in arguing that procreation was in fact an obligation demanded of everyone. Indeed, they regarded it as a divine command:

> No man may abstain from keeping the law "Be fruitful and multiply," [Gen 9:1] unless he already has children: according to the School of Shammai, two sons; according to the School of Hillel, a son and a daughter.[45]

---

[44] B. Ned. 20a-b. However, R. Yoḥanan claims, "People are born lame because [their parents] overturned the table; dumb, because they kiss 'that place'; deaf, because they converse during cohabitation; blind, because they look at 'that place.'" Still, the rabbis reject the complaints of several women who charge that their husbands have "overturned the table," saying that their husbands may do as they please. "Overturned the table" is of course a euphemism. Interestingly, in Greco-Roman erotic art women are frequently seen in the superior position. See the literature in n. 19.
[45] M. Yebam. 6:6.

Not to have children, therefore, is equivalent to shedding blood and diminishing the image of God.[46] Consequently, according to R. Abba, one of the questions to be put to each man when he is led for judgment is "Did you engage in procreation?" The commandment to be fruitful and multiply was in fact so important in the rabbinic traditions that only one rabbi, R. Simeon b. Azzai, was said not to have fulfilled it—and even he argued that his followers should.[47]

To those who chastised R. Simeon for expounding the commandment to be fruitful and multiply without himself seeking to fulfill it, he replied, "my soul is in love with Torah; the world can be carried on by others." This reply reflects an issue which was debated at length by the rabbis—the relation of marriage, procreation, and the study of the Torah. Some argued that marriage was a hindrance to study; others claimed that it was an aid. The primary question, however, was not whether the scholar should marry, but when. The two sides of the debate are reflected in b. Qidd. 29a-b:

> Our Rabbis taught: If one has to study Torah and to marry a
> wife, he should first study and then marry. But if he cannot
> [live] without a wife, he should first marry and then study.
> Rab Judah said in Samuel's name, "The halachah is '[A man]
> first marries and then studies.'" R. Yoḥanan said, "With a
> millstone around the neck shall one study Torah!"

The qualification to the rule that one should study and then marry—"But if he cannot [live] without a wife, he should marry and then study"—suggests that the primary issue of this debate was the ability to control one's sexual urges while engaged in study. That is, according to R. Ḥanina, it is a question of how to study Torah "in purity." Commenting on Ps 19:10 ("the fear of the Lord is pure, enduring forever"), R. Ḥanina says, "This refers to the one who studies the Torah in purity. What does this mean? He marries a woman and afterwards studies the Torah."[48] So, too, R. Ḥuna sends away an unmarried rabbi who has come to study with him, saying, "See to it that you do not appear before me [again] before you are married." This means, according to the Talmud's comment, that R. Ḥuna

---

[46] These interpretations are based on the proximity of the commandment against shedding blood and the phrase "in the image of God made he man" to the commandment to multiply and be fruitful.

[47] B. Yebam. 63a.

[48] B. Yoma 72b.

was in agreement with R. Yoḥanan who said, "He who is twenty years of age and not married spends all of his days in sin."[49] These rabbis argue, therefore, that for the youth engaged in the study of Torah and unable to control his sexual urges, marriage is a means of guarding himself against impurity.

In spite of their emphasis on procreation and their description of marriage as a means for the young scholar to guard himself from impurity, however, it cannot be said that the rabbis had a low opinion of marriage itself. Although there are isolated sayings which refer to marriage as no more than an antidote to immorality,[50] the majority reflect a high regard for it. This view finds a number of expressions in *b. Yebam.* 63a-b. For example,

> R. Eleazar said: A man who has no wife is no proper man; for it is said, "Male and female created he them and called their name Adam."

For R. Eleazar, that is, marriage is part of the created order, which means that the unmarried man is not whole. Other rabbis complete the formula, "A man who has no wife is x" by referring to other Biblical texts, so that the man without a wife is also described as a man without "joy," "blessing," "goodness," and "peace." Another formula the rabbis employ here to emphasize the importance of marriage is "It is preferable to x than to be unmarried." Thus, for example, "It is preferable to live in grief than to dwell in widowhood." Perhaps the most interesting saying which reflects the rabbis' high regard for marriage, however, comes from elsewhere in the Talmud. In *b. Sanh.* 22a R. Abba b. Ibo says, "Forty days before the embryo is formed, a heavenly voice goes forth and says: The daughter of so and so for so and so." At least some of the rabbis, that is, even ascribed to the belief that "marriages are made in heaven."

The sayings on divorce in the rabbinic literature provide further evidence of the high regard in which the rabbis held marriage. For although divorce was allowed, and although the reasons for which it was granted sometimes seem lax,[51] there are a number of sayings which demonstrate

---

[49] *B. Qidd.* 29b.
[50] *B. Yebam.* 63a attributes to R. Ḥiyya the saying, "All we can expect of [our wives] is that they bring up our children and keep us from sin." See also *b. Sanh.* 76a and *b. Qidd.* 29b.
[51] The well-known debate between the Schools of Hillel and Shammai is discussed below.

that divorce was viewed as a lamentable end to marriage. For example, *b. Sanh.* 2a attributes to R. Shaman b. Abba the saying, "Come and see with what reluctance is divorce granted; King David was permitted *yihud*,[52] yet not divorce." More pointedly, *Gittin*, the tractate of the Babylonian Talmud dealing with divorce, concludes its discussion with the saying, "He who dismisseth his wife is hated by God."[53]

This survey has shown that the issues addressed in the literature of the apocrypha and pseudepigrapha continued to concern the shapers of Jewish life and thought in the rabbinic era, even though on occasion the focus of the discussion shifted somewhat. There were, however, other issues which attracted the greater attention of the rabbis and consequently reflect more precisely their own concerns. Many of the sayings which address these new issues were codified by the editors of the Mishnah in the division Nashim. Jacob Neusner has shown that this division has its own internal coherence and therefore must be analyzed as a system, if one is to avoid distorting it.[54] Since, however, the purpose of the present essay is to understand the development of marriage rules in the letters of Paul, it is not necessary to look at the division as a whole, for it reflects the concerns of a later period. Instead, we will concentrate our attention on the sayings attributed to sages of the period prior to 70 C.E., hoping to discover the significance of the rules for this period. Neusner himself has in fact isolated this period and analysed the sayings which derive from it. His identification of the early traditions will be the basis of our treatment here.

Among the sayings attributed to the pre-70 sages, five topics dealing with marriage tend to recur: (1) persons with whom one is permitted to marry; (2) testimonies regarding the status of persons desiring to marry; (3) divorce; (4) property rights of married and betrothed persons; and (5) abstinence from sexual intercourse. These sayings occur primarily in the Division Nashim and the tractate Niddah, but doublets and additional sayings are scattered throughout the Mishnah.

(1) As we have seen, the Schools of Hillel and Shammai agreed that the prohibition against intermarriage with the seven nations of Deuteronomy 7 should be extended to include all foreigners. However, to the extent that evidence allows us to determine, this was not a pressing issue for the pre-70 sages. Their attention was focused more on the question of

---

[52]Private association between a man and a woman, in this case between David and Abishag. See 1 Kings 1:1-4.

[53]*B. Giṭ.* 90b.

[54]1980, vol 5.

marriage among Jews themselves. Two issues were especially important: (a) levirate marriage and (b) intermarriage between persons of the priestly and non-priestly castes.

(a) Regarding levirate marriage, it is enough to note here that the Schools of Hillel and Shammai each prohibited the levir from marrying women which the other permitted him to marry. Consequently, some marriages allowed by one School would be considered invalid by the other. The significance of this debate apparently stems from the questionable legitimacy of the offspring of invalid marriages.

(b) In the Ushan period (ca 140-170 C.E.), the rabbis distinguish ten separate groups within Judaism, tracing their emergence to the period of the return to Jerusalem from Babylonian captivity.[55] These groups were ranked according to degrees of purity and classified for purposes of intermarriage. In the period prior to 70, however, the sages appear to recognize only two groups: priests (and members of priestly families) and all other Jews.

Lev 21:13-14 decrees that the high priest should marry a virgin from his own people and that he is forbidden to marry a widow, a divorced woman, or a harlot. The regular order of priests, however, was only forbidden marriage with a divorced woman or a harlot. In the period with which we are dealing, these rules appear to have been strictly applied. Indeed, in m. Ketub. 2:9, even a woman from a priestly family is declared ineligible for marriage with a priest if the city in which she lives is captured by a foreign army—unless, that is, she has disinterested witnesses who can testify that she had not been raped, and thus made impure. According to m. ᶜEd. 8:2, however, some families in the priestly circle appear to have avoided even the hint of such profanation. Here, although R. Jose the High Priest and R. Zechariah b. ha-Kaddab are said to have testified on behalf of a young woman who had been held as a pledge in the free city of Ashkelon, the woman's family ostracized her and thus assured her ineligibility for marriage with a priest. For the sages prior to 70, therefore, the question of whom one may marry was as much concerned with those within the community as with those outside.

(2) The two passages from the Mishnah just cited illustrate the concern with testimonies dealing with a woman's suitability for marriage. This issue had special significance in the case of widows. The debate focused on whether a widow returning from "beyond the sea" may marry again and receive her ketubah (her dowry) on the basis of her own testimony that

---

[55]M. Qidd. 4:1.

her husband is dead. Although the School of Hillel initially rejected both the ruling that she may remarry and receive her *ketubah* and the interpretation of the tradition which underlies the ruling, the Mishnah reports that the Shammaites were convincing in their argument in favor of it so that the Hillelites changed their opinion and followed them.[56]

(3) Regarding divorce, there was again a debate between the School of Hillel and the School of Shammai. The debate focused on the interpretation of ערות דבר ("something indecent") in Deut 24:1. According to *m. Git.* 9:10 the Shammaites interpreted this strictly in terms of sexual immorality, while the Hillelites took it more broadly, so that a man may divorce his wife "even if she spoiled a dish for him." *M. Ketub.* 13:5 provides an interesting sidelight to the question of divorce in the pre-70 period, for it addresses the woman's rights in the event that the man to whom she is betrothed refuses to marry her.[57] It attributes to Admon, one of the pre-Tannaitic sages, a ruling that if the father of a woman is unable to pay his prospective son-in-law a sum of money promised in the writ of betrothal and the man consequently refuses to marry her, she may say to him, "Had I myself undertaken it, I would sit down [and remain unmarried] until my hair grows gray; but since now it is my father that undertook it because of me, what can I do? Either marry me or set me free."

(4) The mishnah just cited illustrates that the pre-70 sages address themselves to financial questions deriving from marriage contracts. Indeed, since the *ketubah* was essentially a financial contract, it is not surprising that such questions were frequently discussed. The specific rulings of this period which survive in the Mishnah deal with three related issues: the rights of inheritance as they related to a widow and her husband's heirs,[58] a woman's property rights before marriage and in the event of divorce,[59] and a woman's property rights between the death of her husband and levirate marriage.[60] It is enough to note for our purposes that while the Schools generally agreed that once married the husband exercised authority over his wife's property, they debated the extent to which she was independent prior to marriage and after the end of her marriage.

---

[56] *M. Yebam.* 15:1-3. See also 16:7.

[57] In order for a woman to marry someone other than the man to whom she is betrothed, she must obtain a writ of divorce.

[58] *M. Git.* 4:3; *m. B. Bat.* 9:8-9.

[59] *M. Ketub.* 8:1, 13:1-3.

[60] *M. Yebam.*, 4:3-4.

(5) In the debate concerning abstinence from sexual intercourse, two issues are addressed: times in which a couple *may* abstain and times in which they *must* abstain. According to *m. Ketub.* 5:6, the School of Shammai ruled that a man may abstain from sexual intercourse with his wife for two weeks; while the School of Hillel ruled that he may abstain for only one week. Both schools agree, however, that the husband must obtain his wife's consent. In the event that a man abstains from sexual intercourse without his wife's consent (or if a woman abstains without her husband's consent), penalties were adduced: If the husband refuses his wife, her *ketubah* may be increased three denars for every week; if the wife refuses her husband, he may reduce her *ketubah* seven denars for every week.[61] The only reason for which a man may abstain from sexual relations without his wife's consent is to study Torah. But this exemption is granted only to the disciples of the sages and for a period of no more than thirty days.[62]

The time during which a husband and wife *must* abstain from sexual relations is the period of her *niddah*, her menstrual impurity. A whole tractate of the Mishnah's Division of Purities is in fact devoted to the question of *niddah*, the basis of which is found in Lev 15:19-30 and 12:1-8. The sayings of this tractate attributed to the pre-70 sages deal with how a woman determines when her impurity begins and ends;[63] types of clean and unclean blood;[64] rules of *niddah* as they relate to the first night of marriage;[65] and restrictions of the wife's daily chores during the period of her uncleanness.[66]

When one turns to the sages' discussion of these five topics after examining the treatment of marriage and sexual morality in the other Jewish traditions, the differences come into clear focus. The traditions of the apocrypha and pseudepigrapha define the Jewish community by contrasting the moral values of Jews and Gentiles in sharply polemical terms. We are moral; they are immoral. We honor the sanctity of marriage; they dishonor it. We abstain from homosexual acts; they are renowned for practicing them. As we have seen, there are traces of this kind of polemic in the rabbinic literature also. But the emphasis lies elsewhere, at least for the pre-70 sages. For them the differing moral values of Jews and

---

[61]*M. Ketub.* 5:7.
[62]*M. Ketub.* 5:6.
[63]*M. Nid.* 1:1, 2:4. See also *m. 'Ed.* 1:1.
[64]*M. Nid.* 2:6.
[65]*M. Nid.* 10:1.
[66]*M. Nid.* 10:6, 8.

Gentiles apparently needed little exposition. Thus, they define the Jewish
community not by contrasting it to the surrounding world, but by carefully
regulating all aspects of its internal order, including marriage. Consequently, marriage rules are not important in the definition of the Jewish
community in and of themselves, but as one part of the larger system
which determines every aspect of day-to-day life within it. And it is in
the development of this system that one sees the difference between the
traditions of the apocrypha and pseudepigrapha on the one hand and those
of the sages on the other. The one is concerned primarily with defining
the community, the other with ordering it.

Now, to those familiar with Paul's treatment of marriage and sexual
morality, it will be clear why I have dealt here with such issues as the
distinction between Jew and Gentile, divorce, abstinence from sexual
intercourse, and the remarriage of widows. Paul discusses all of these.[67]
It may be less clear, however, why I have treated issues such as niddah
and levirate marriage. Paul discusses neither. I have done so because I
maintain that to determine the significance of Paul's treatment of marriage and sexual morality it is as important to know what he does not
discuss as it is to know what he does discuss. Thus, since in 1 Thess 4:3-8
Paul is concerned with distinguishing between believers and "the Gentiles
who do not know God," it would appear he addresses himself to defining
the community, just as the Jewish moralists of the diaspora had done.
Since, however, in 1 Corinthians 7 he dealt with issues such as divorce,
whether one should marry, abstinence from sexual intercourse, and the
remarriage of widows, it would appear that, in this letter at least, he was
also concerned with ordering the community, just as the sages were. But
his failure to treat niddah and levirate marriage indicates that Paul deals
with ordering the community in ways quite different from the sages.

No doubt one reason Paul does not treat these two issues is that in
1 Corinthians 7 he is addressing questions sent to him by the Corinthian
community,[68] which, being predominantly Gentile, would have accorded
little importance to rules of niddah and levirate marriage. More important, however, Paul himself doubtless considered niddah and levirate
marriage issues which, like circumcision, had nothing to do with believing
the gospel. Still, since in his efforts to order the Corinthian community
Paul does treat topics addressed by the sages, it is important to note the
ones he does not treat. This will highlight the issues he did consider

---

[67]Though Paul of course is concerned with distinguishing between
believers and Gentiles and not between Jews and Gentiles.
[68]See 1 Cor 7:1.

important and consequently help us in determining the significance of the way he treats them.

But before we look at Paul himself, we must examine the other moral traditions prevalent in the world he knew. Paul was a Jew. But he was a Jew who lived and worked in cities dominated by Hellenistic culture. And it is to be expected that he was aware of, and even influenced by, the attitudes toward marriage and sexual morality held by that culture. In order to determine the significance of Paul's treatment of these issues, therefore, we must also have a clear understanding of the value accorded to them by the dominant culture, especially by those who claimed to be the guardians of its moral conduct.

2

Marriage Precepts in the Greco-Roman Moral Traditions

In recent years a number of scholars, taking up the work of a previous generation, have shown just how much Paul was at home in the Greco-Roman world.[1] He spoke its language, lived in its cities, and knew its culture. One aspect of Paul's knowledge of Greco-Roman culture was his familiarity with many of the *topoi* current in philosophical and rhetorical circles,[2] among which was the *topos* περὶ γάμου. We cannot offer a detailed analysis of this *topos* here, but it is important to examine some of the issues treated in it, since at several points the examples of the *topos* bear striking resemblance to Paul's treatment of marriage, especially in 1 Corinthians 7.

---

[1] Malherbe 1977b, chaps. 1-2 and Keck 1974 provide critical surveys of the earlier literature and outline the course of current research in this area. See also Smith 1975, Meeks 1975, Gager 1975 (all, with Keck's article, growing out of the SBL's working group on the social world of Early Christianity) and Theissen 1975a. The most comprehensive treatment of Paul in the Greco-Roman world now is Meeks 1983. Other important studies include Theissen 1974a, 1974b, 1975b, and Sampley 1980. (Theissen's work has been collected and translated by John Schütz in Theissen 1982.) See also now the Epilogue in Malherbe 1983b, which surveys recent literature dealing with the social world of early Christianity.

[2] On the question of Paul's use of *topoi*, see Bradley 1953 and Mullins 1980. My understanding of *topos*, however, is broader than the one developed in these two articles. Recent studies examining in more detail Paul's use of particular *topoi* include Hock 1980, Betz 1979, and Bartchy 1973. Malherbe 1968, 1970, 1983a, and the forthcoming article "Hellenistic Moralists and the New Testament" are ground-breaking for understanding the paraenetic aspect of Paul's letters. Malherbe demonstrates that much of Paul's language and many of his metaphors are common to the moral traditions.

It was the Stoics who developed the περὶ γάμου *topos* most fully.[3] But
we must not limit our discussion to them alone, for many of the arguments they used or spoke against already had a long history. Some were
also taken up by other moral traditions, most notably the Peripatetic,
Neo-Pythagorean, and Middle-Platonic.[4] Moreover, the evidence suggests
that some of the concerns voiced by the philosophers were shared by
people outside the philosophical schools, for they also appear in New
Comedy, inscriptions, marriage contracts, romances, and in political
speeches—such as those attributed to Tiberius by the Roman historian Dio
Cassius.[5]

Among the issues treated in the *topos On Marriage* and which attract
the concern of others outside philosophical circles, four stand out because
of the frequency with which they recur: whether marriage is desirable
(especially for the wise man); whom one should marry; relations between
husbands and wives; and the significance of producing children. We take
these up now, not simply to clarify specific elements in Paul's treatment
of marriage, but also to set his views in historical and social context. We
will see that although Greco-Roman society is frequently described as
immoral and licentious, there were in fact many who held marriage and
family life in very high regard, discussing in detail their importance for
society.

WHETHER MARRIAGE IS DESIRABLE

Many of the pre-Socratic philosophers disdained marriage. Plutarch and
Stobaeus, for example, recount a story of Thales, who, when young,
refused to marry because "it is not yet time" and, when older, refused to
marry because "it is no longer time."[6] According to Stobaeus, Thales's

---

[3]On the origin of the *topos On Marriage* see Praechter 1901, Exkursus
2, 121-131. Praechter provides a review and critique of previous attempts
to determine the origin of the *topos*. He concludes that while some
aspects of the *topos* are traceable to earlier philosophers, the shape of the
topos itself was the product of the Stoa.

[4]Gaiser 1974, 59-83 provides a valuable annotated bibliography of
ancient sources on marriage. Balch 1981 and 1983 also contain a wealth of
material on this topic. I have learned much from Balch's work and from
conversations with him.

[5]Older works such as Friedländer 1913 and Preisker 1927 list many
references to this kind of evidence.

[6]Plutarch *Table Talk* 3.63 (*Moralia* 654C); Stobaeus 4.520, 4-5.

reason for not marrying and having children was that "[he] did not wish to subject life to voluntary griefs."[7] Solon sounded a similar note when he argued that a woman is a burden which is hard to bear (χάλεπον φορτίον ἡ γυνή).[8] Antiphon developed this argument further, claiming that marriage is a "great struggle" (μέγας ἀγών)[9] and suggesting that even in the good things of married life one finds "the most grievous things" (τὸ λυπηρόν), since "pleasures do not travel by themselves, but griefs and burdens (λυπαὶ καὶ πόνοι) follow them."[10] Taking a wife, he concludes, simply doubles a man's worries, and children multiply them, so that a married man's life is "full of care" (φροντίδων πλέα).[11]

The two most famous of the critics of married life prior to the formulation of the topos On Marriage, however, were Epicurus and Diogenes. Epicurus, whose view was attacked explicitly by Epictetus, stated that although the wise man might marry "owing to special circumstances in his life" (κατὰ περίστασιν βίου), as a general rule he would not marry and raise a family—just as he would not participate in politics.[12] To do so would distract him from the pursuit of pleasure and prevent him from obtaining calmness of soul (ἀταραξία). Diogenes, whose attitude was also the topic of later discussion,[13]

> would praise those who were about to marry and refrained, those who intending to go on a voyage never set sail, those who thinking to engage in politics do no such thing, those also

References to Stobaeus cite volume, page, and line of the Hense edition. Diogenes Laertius (Lives 6.54) attributes a similar saying to Diogenes of Sinope: "Being asked what was the right time to marry, Diogenes replied: 'For the young man not yet; for the old man never at all'" (trans. Hicks. Loeb ed.).
[7]Stobaeus 4.521, 9-11 Hense.
[8]Stobaeus 4.521, 5-7.
[9]On Harmony (περὶ ὁμονοίας) 357, 15-16. Text and German translation in Diels 1954, vol. 2. References are to page and line of this edition. The English translations are my own.
[10]On Harmony 358, 7-11 Diels.
[11]On Harmony 360, 1.
[12]Diog. Laer. Lives 10.118-119. See also Jerome Against Jovian 1.48. Text of Jerome in Migne 23, cols. 276-278; there is an Eng. trans. in Fremantle 1893, 383-384. Epictetus's rebuttal will be taken up below.
[13]To argue that griefs always accompany pleasure was common in discussions of married life. See, for example, Tiberius's speech in Cassius Dio's Roman History 56.8.2-4.

34 Not like the Gentiles

who purposing to rear a family do not do so, and those who
make ready to live with potentates, yet never come near
them after all.[14]

Such conventions, he held, were not in keeping with the goals of the wise
man, "self-sufficiency" (αὐτάρκεια) and simplicity of life (ἄσκησις).
There were, of course, positive evaluations of marriage prior to the
development of the topos On Marriage. Socrates married, providing later
philosophers with support for the view that even marriage with a shrewish
wife is preferable to no marriage at all.[15] Both Plato and Aristotle discuss marriage in the context of their treatment of the ideal state, arguing
that it has its proper place in society.[16] Since their views have been
treated in detail elsewhere,[17] we need note here only that several of their
arguments find their way into the Stoic topos On Marriage.[18] One of the
most important favorable analyses of marriage prior to the development
of the topos On Marriage is Xenophon's treatment of the division of labor
within marriage in his treatise Concerning Household Management. Its
basic premise—that men are stronger and thus better suited to outside
work while women are weaker and better suited to inside work—is fundamental for almost all later discussion of the relation between husbands
and wives.[19] Xenophon's discussion, of course, presupposes that marriage
is desirable.

Significantly, many positive evaluations of marriage derive from the
early Cynic-Stoic tradition. Diogenes Laertius reports that in his Republic
Zeno maintained that the wise man would marry and beget children.[20]
Jerome ridicules Chrysippus for advocating that the wise man marry so

[14]Diog. Laer. Lives 6.54. Trans. Hicks. Loeb ed.
[15]Musonius Rufus, Is Marriage a Handicap for the Pursuit of Philosophy? Text and translation in Lutz 1947. The reference here is p. 90, lines
25ff. See also Epictetus To Those Who Fear Want 3.26.23.
[16]For Plato's treatment of marriage see primarily Rep. 5, 459D-461E
and Laws 6.771E-783B. For Aristotle, see Pol 1 and NE 8.
[17]See Balch 1981, 23-26; 33-38. Balch demonstrates their significance
for understanding the development of the household codes which appear in
the New Testament.
[18]See van Geytenbeek 1963, 53ff. and Praechter 1901, 66-90 and 121-
127.
[19]Xenophon offers a detailed analysis of this division in Concerning
Household Management 7.3-10.13. For parallels in later philosophers, see
the works cited in nn. 17-18.
[20]Lives 7.121.

that he would not outrage Jupiter and the gods of marriage and birth.[21] Crates, the Cynic philosopher, married—a fact that is frequently noted by later proponents of marriage.[22] Moreover, one of the earliest references to the *topos On Marriage* comes from this early period, Cleanthes's περὶ ὑμεναίου.[23]

The first indication that marriage had become a formal topic of debate is Theophrastus's treatise *On Marriage*.[24] It is not clear whether Theophrastus directed this treatise against Cleanthes specifically, but its opposition to the arguments which appear in later Stoic examples of the *topos* suggests that he had the Stoic view in mind.[25]

Theophrastus admits that if the right conditions are fulfilled (namely, "that the wife . . . be fair, of good character, and honest parentage, the husband in good health and ample means"), the wise man may marry. But since these conditions seldom obtain, in his opinion, he argues that a wise man should not take a wife. Two arguments were especially weighty for Theophrastus: (1) "[The wise man's] study of philosophy will be hindered, [since] it is impossible for anyone to attend to his books and his wife;"[26] and (2) "to marry for the sake of children, so that our name may not perish, or that we may have support in old age, and leave our property without dispute, is the height of stupidity."[27]

Concerning the first argument Theophrastus discusses at length the ways a wife is a burden (*sarcina*) to the wise man. He maintains, for example, that she is hard to support if she is poor and torture if she is rich; moreover, one always has to praise her beauty, lest she think you are looking at another woman. And if she *is* beautiful everyone will desire her; while if she is ugly she is not worth having in the first place. To those who claim that one should marry to get a manager for the household Theophrastus counters that a faithful slave can do this better than a wife. And to those who argue that one should marry "to solace weariness, to banish solitude" he rejoins that a slave can tend the sick better than a wife, without driving one to "the distraction of despair" by constantly boasting

---

[21] *Against Jovian* I.48. References to column in Migne.

[22] See, for example, Musonius *Is Marriage a Handicap?* 92.4-6 Lutz.

[23] See the list of Cleanthes's works in Diog. Lear. *Lives* 7.175.

[24] The treatise is quoted at length by Jerome in *Against Jovian* 1.47.

[25] See Praechter 1901, 121-127.

[26] 276 Migne. Trans. Fremantle 1893.

[27] 278.

of her anxiety.[28] And the concern with solitude is misguided, he argues, since

> the wise man can never be alone. He has with him the good men of all time, and turns his mind [to them] freely whenever he chooses. What is inaccessible to him in person he can embrace in thought. And if men are scarce he converses with God. He is never less alone than when alone.[29]

To marry for the sake of children is ill advised, Theophrastus maintains, because it is by no means certain that children will outlive their parents. Consequently, there is no guarantee of their supporting them in old age. Moreover, what difference does it make to a dead man how his possessions are used? "Indeed, the surest way of having a good heir," Theophrastus argues, "is to ruin your fortune in a good cause while you live."[30]

As indicated earlier, the views of the later Stoics—Antipater, Musonius, Hierocles, and Epictetus—are opposite to those of Theophrastus at almost every point.[31] They argue that marriage *is* desirable and that a wife and children *are* helpful to a man—running the household, taking care of him in old age, and setting him free for the pursuit of philosophy. The Stoics have another reason for marrying also, one which sets the debate in a new context. They argue that marriage not only frees one for the study of philosophy but also for taking part in political affairs. Indeed, concern for the *polis* is primary for them. Without marriage, they argue, there will be no lawful children, and without children the cities will perish.

Although Antipater's is the first of the later Stoic *topoi* on marriage, Hierocles's treatise *On Marriage* is more developed and thus serves better to illustrate the scope of the Stoic defense of marriage. Hierocles begins

---

[28]277.

[29]278.

[30]278.

[31]For the following discussion: The text of Antipater is from von Arnim 1921, vol. 3, 254-257. References cite page and line of this edition. The translations are my own. (There is a German translation in Gaiser 1974, 36-39.) The text of Hierocles is from Stobaeus 4.502.1-507.5 of the Hense edition. References cite volume, page, and line of this edition. I have used the English translation of Taylor 1822, 95-105. Text and translation of Musonius Rufus from Lutz 1947. For Epictetus I have used the Loeb ed., trans. Oldfather.

his essay by demonstrating the importance of marriage for the survival of the *polis*. "The whole of our race," he writes, "is naturally adapted to society" (πρὸς κοινωνίαν) and marriage is "the first and most elementary of all associations" (πρώτη δὲ καὶ στοιχειωδεστάτη τῶν κοινωνίων).[32] In practical terms this means for Hierocles that "cities cannot exist without households" and that households must be headed by married persons, for the household of a married man is "imperfect" (ἡμιτελής), while that of a married man is "perfect and full" (τέλειος καὶ πλήρης).[33] Hierocles stresses the relation between marriage and politics even more when he discusses marriage and producing children:[34]

> We are ... loudly called upon by our country to [marry and procreate children]. For we do not beget children so much for ourselves as for our country, procuring a race that may follow us, and supplying the community with our successors.[35]

Having dealt with the importance of marriage for the *polis*, Hierocles turns to more personal reasons for viewing marriage as desirable. First, he argues, marriage is a matter of prime importance (προηγούμενος)[36] for the wise man (τῷ σοφῷ). He avoids it only if "particular circumstances require it" (κατὰ περίστασιν).[37] Since, therefore, ordinary men should

---

[32]4.502,3-4 Hense.

[33]4.502,5-7.

[34]4.604,26-605,3. It is not clear whether this segment (603,9-605,16) is part of the *topos On Marriage* which has been separated by Stobaeus according to his own subject matter or is a distinct *topos*. It beings "In the *topos On Marriage and Producing Children*, a discussion *On Producing Many Children* has been included" ('Εν δὲ τῷ περὶ τοῦ γάμου καὶ τῆς παιδοποιίας τοπῷ θετέος ἐστὶ καὶ ὁ τῆς πολυτεκνίας λόγος). My trans. On this see Praechter 1901, 66-67. For our purposes, it makes no difference whether this is a separate *topos* or part of the *topos On Marriage*. The subject matter is essentially the same. Indeed, as we shall see, producing children was one of the primary issues involved in the question whether one should marry.

[35]4.604,26-605,3 Hense.

[36]4.502,7-8. Taylor translates, "Wedlock is to be precedaneously chosen." Hierocles refers here to his argument in another treatise, *On Households* (περὶ οἴκων).

[37]4.502,9 Hense. This is exactly the opposite of Theophrastus's argument. See above p 35. Hierocles also allowed for extenuating circumstances in the treatment of one's parents. "With regard to the souls of our parents, we should, in the first place, procure for them hilarity; which will

imitate (μιμεῖσθαι) the wise man, they too should marry, "unless some circumstance occurs to prevent it from taking place" (εἰ γὲ μὴ τις εἴη περίστασις ἐμπωδών).[38]

Second, Hierocles holds that nature (ἡ φύσις), which has in fact exhorted the wise man to marry, decrees that man should marry, having made him "gregarious" (συναγελαστικός) and "adapted to copulation" (συνδυαστικός). Nature has also made "the procreation of children and the stability of life" to be "the one and common work of wedlock" (ἐν τὲ καὶ κοινὸν ἔργον).[39] And finally, nature teaches that every creature must live according to its constitution (ὅτι τῇ παρ᾽ αὐτῆς κατασκευῇ σύμφω-νον τὴν ἐκλογὴν χρὴ γίγνεσθαι τῶν καθηκόντων).[40] Since this means that "it is not possible to conceive of a governor without the governed, nor of the governed without a governor," marriage, in which the man governs and the woman is governed, is part of the natural constitution of mankind.[41]

Third, Hierocles maintains that marriage is "advantageous" (σύμφο-ρος).[42] First (πρῶτον), it is advantageous because it produces "divine fruit" (καρπὸν θεῖον), children, who are "allies" when their parents are young and active and "helpers" when their parents are old and sick.[43] Second (ἔπειτα), even before children are born, married life is advanta-geous because a wife is a comfort to her husband. She helps him to forget the cares (μέριμνα) of the world and the occupations which are necessary to life (οἱ ἀναγκαῖοι περισπασμοί) and is a helpmate for him, providing sacrifices for festivals, running the household when he is away on busi-ness, looking after the servants, and taking care of him when he is sick.[44]

And fourth, Hierocles argues that married life is "beautiful" (καλός).[45] The adornment (κόσμος) of a household is not in the decorations of the

---

be especially obtained if we are conversant with them by night and by day, unless something prevents us (εἰ μὴ τι κωλύοι) . . ." Stobaeus 4.643,3-6 Hense. Trans. Taylor 1822, 87.
[38]4.502,9-12 Hense.
[39]4.502,15-19. Musonius uses much of the same argument in Is Mar-riage a Handicap? 92,6-20.
[40]4.502,21-22.
[41]4.503,12-16. On the relation of this argument to Xenophon's Con-cerning Household Management, see Balch 1981, 23-62.
[42]4.503,18 Hense.
[43]4.503,19-24. See Musonius Should Every Child that is Born be Raised? 98,1-2, where he argues that "raising many children is an honorable and profitable thing" (καλὸν καὶ λυσιτέλες).
[44]4,503,24-505,4 Hense.
[45]4,505,5.

building, but in the "communion" (κοινωνία) of husband and wife,[46] which Hierocles describes as a "yoking" (ζεῦγος) of the two.[47] It involves their being linked by fate (συγκαθειμαρμένοι); dedicated to the gods of marriage, of births, and of the household (καθειρωμένοι θεοῖς γαμηλίοις γενεθλίοις ἐφεστίοις); in accord with one another (συμφωνοῦντοι ἀλλή-λοις); "holding all things in common, as far as to their bodies, or rather their souls themselves" (πάντα κοινὰ πεποιημένοι μέχρι καὶ τῶν σωμά-των, μᾶλλον δὲ καὶ αὐτῶν τῶν ψυχῶν); and looking after the household in a moderate and appropriate way.[48]

Hierocles next turns to a refutation of those who claim that marriage is "burdensome and grievous" (βαρὺς ἢ φορτίον).[49] He counters that a wife is not a burden at all; on the contrary, a wife makes burdens easier to bear. "There is not anything so troublesome," he argues, "which will not be easily borne by a husband and wife when they are concordant, and are willing to endure it in common."[50] Only those who have not married "for the sake of having children and the relationship of a wife," but for a large dowry, or beauty, or some such reason, experience marriage as burdensome. For they gain a tyrant rather than a wife and find themselves pitted in a constant struggle for superiority.[51]

Thus, Hierocles insists, marriage is not bad in and of itself. It is burdensome only to those who are imprudent, and for such persons all things are a burden.[52] Indeed, marriage and the benefits it affords, he repeats in concluding, are given to men by nature (παρὰ τῆς φύσεως), by the laws (παρὰ τῶν νόμων), and by the gods (παρὰ τῶν θεῶν).[53]

It is not necessary to outline in such detail the other Stoic treatises dealing with marriage, since Hierocles includes almost all the arguments

---

[46] 4.505,5-7.
[47] 4.505,12.
[48] 4.505,12-20. Hierocles's argument that married persons hold all things in common was an important one for the Stoics. Antipater says of husbands and wives that only they have in common "not only their property and the things that are nearest and dearest to all men—namely, their children and their souls—but also their bodies" (256,16-18 von Arnim, my trans.). Musonius echoes this, maintaining that only in the relationship between husbands and wives does one find "everything judged to be common, body, soul, and possessions" (94,8-9 Lutz).
[49] "I have frequently wondered at those who conceive that the life with a woman is burdensome and grievous" (4.505,22-24 Hense. Trans. Taylor 1844, 100).
[50] 4.505,24-506.3 Hense.
[51] 4.506,13-22.
[52] 4.506,26-507,5.
[53] 4.506,26-507.5

40   Not like the Gentiles

that occur in them. But because they were so important for the Stoic view of marriage, two of his arguments do deserve closer examination: marriage and the pursuit of philosophy and marriage and the survival of the *polis.*

Antipater also argues that a wife is a great help to her husband. Like Hierocles, he says that she will take care of the household and attend him when he is sick.[54] But he is more specific than Hierocles when arguing that a wife frees one for the pursuit of philosophy. He claims that acquiring a wife is like acquiring another pair of hands, so that "being two instead of one [the man who marries] will accomplish more in life."[55] Thus, he concludes,

> for the gentleman who wishes to have leisure for study (περὶ τοὺς λόγους) or political affairs (τὰ πολιτικὰ ἔργα), or both, [married life] is absolutely necessary (lit. perfectly unalterable). For the more he goes out from the house, the more he ought to take to his side someone to take care of the house and make himself free from every day cares (περὶ τὰ ἀναγκαῖα ἀπερίσπαστος).[56]

Musonius is also very specific in dealing with this issue. In fact, one of his diatribes is addressed to it: *Is Marriage a Handicap for the Pursuit of Philosophy?* (τι ἐμπόδιον τῷ φιλοσοφεῖν γάμος). His answer is an unequivocal No. He points out that marriage was not a handicap to Pythagoras and Socrates, and asks how it can be a handicap to those who have a home and servants, when someone like Crates could marry in spite of his self-imposed poverty.[57] Interestingly, however, although Musonius clearly knows of the tradition dividing the indoor and outdoor work between men and women, and can even speak of a wife as a "great help" (μέγα ὄφελος) to her husband,[58] he does not use Antipater's argument that a wife frees her husband for the pursuit of philosophy—perhaps because he thought that wives too should be engaged in this pursuit.

Epictetus's view of marriage and philosophy was more complex. He maintains that most men should marry, but says nothing of the value of a wife in running the household, of the love between husband and wife, or of

---

[54]255,28-31 von Arnim; see also 256,24-25.
[55]256,25-26. My trans.
[56]256,34-257.4. My trans.
[57]90.1-92.6 Lutz.
[58]*That Women Too Should Study Philosophy* 42,9. Earlier he had argued, "In the first place, a woman must be a good housekeeper, that is a careful accountant of all that pertains to the welfare of her house and capable of directing the household slaves" (40,10-12. Trans. Lutz).

their holding all things in common. As we shall see, his only concern is with the obligations of citizenship.[59] In contrast to Epictetus's view of marriage for mankind in general, however, stands his position with regard to the Ideal Cynic. He should *not* marry, for "in such an order of things as the present, which is like a battle field (ὡς ἐν παρατάξει), it is a question, perhaps, if the Cynic ought not to be free from distraction (ἀπερίσπαστον), wholly devoted to the service of God."[60] Among the distractions he mentions are the duties to one's wife, children, and in-laws.[61] Thus, while Antipater and Hierocles see marriage as a way of becoming free from the distraction of running a household so that one may pursue study or politics, for Epictetus marriage and the duties it implies are the distractions from which one must be freed in order to pursue philosophy, or more precisely for the service of God.

MARRIAGE AND CIVIC RESPONSIBILITIES

Like Hierocles, Antipater also begins his treatise *On Marriage* by speaking of marriage as a civic responsibility. He refers to it as "one of the necessities of life, indeed an obligation of the first order" (τῶν ἀναγκαιοτάτων καὶ πρώτων καθηκόντων).[62] Thus, he encourages "the noble and courageous youth" who is "cultured and civic-minded" (ὁ εὐγενὴς καὶ εὔψυχος νέος, ἔτι δ' ἥμερος καὶ πολιτικός) to marry and produce children for their homeland.[63]

---

[59]The only two instances which reflect the arguments of earlier treatises are in his discourses *To Those Who Fear Want* (3.26) and *Of Providence* (1.6). In the former Epictetus argues that poverty was not a deterrent to marrying, since Socrates, who lived with little, had a wife and children (3.26.23). This, however, is a secondary argument. Epictetus's primary concern is not with marriage but the fear of poverty. Diogenes, who, as we have seen, disdained marriage, is one of the other examples Epictetus cites of philosophers who lived with little. In the latter discourse, Epictetus maintains that "the passion of [male and female] for intercourse with the other, and the faculty which makes use of the organs which have been constructed for this purpose" are proofs for the existence of divine providence (1.6.8-9. Trans. Oldfather). This echoes Hierocles's argument concerning the place of marriage in the natural order. Epictetus, however, does not speak here of marriage, but simply of sexual desire.

[60]3.22,69. One in fact takes up the Cynic way of life only at the call of God (3.22,2, 23, 36, and 53).

[61]3.22,70-71.

[62]255,5 von Arnim. My trans.

Musonius echoes this, asking

> Is it fitting for each man to act for himself alone or to act in
> the interest of his neighbor also, not only that there be homes
> in the city, but also that the city may not be deserted and
> that the common good may best be served?[64]

Indeed, Musonius refers to marriage as the first line of defense for the
city's protection. "Whoever destroys marriage," he argues, "destroys the
home, the city, and the whole human race."[65]

Epictetus is even more adamant. In the discourse *A Conversation with
the Imperial Bailiff of the Free Cities, who was an Epicurean* he ridicules
the Epicureans for being inconsistent and neglecting their duties. On the
question of marriage he charges:

> In the name of God, I ask you, can you imagine an Epicurean
> State: One man says, "I do not marry." "Neither do I," says
> another, "for people ought not to marry." No, nor have chil-
> dren; no, nor perform the duties of a citizen. And what, do
> you suppose, will happen then? Where are the citizens to
> come from? Who will educate them? Who will be super-
> intendent of the ephebi, or gymnasium director? Yes, and
> what will either of these teach them? What the young men of
> Lacedaemon or Athens were taught? Take me a young man;
> bring him up according to your doctrines. Your doctrines are
> bad, subversive of the State, destructive of the family, not
> even fit for women. Drop these doctrines, man. You live in an
> imperial State; it is your duty to hold office, to judge
> uprightly, to keep your hands off the property of other
> people; no woman but your wife ought to look handsome to
> you, no boy handsome, no silver plate handsome, no gold
> plate.[66]

---

[63]254,25-31. He argues that after all it is more important for cities to
grow than for flocks and herds to grow. It is striking that although
Antipater does not encourage marriage as a guard against sexual immorality, he is concerned with "the weakness, anarchy, and inclination to
sensual pleasure and the easy life" that obtains in cities. My trans.

[64]*Is Marriage a Handicap?* 92,17-20 Lutz.

[65]*Is Marriage a Handicap?* 92,34-38.

[66]3.7,19-22.

He continues, insisting that men should be honored not for their wealth, but for "the principal duties themselves" (τὰ δ' αὐτὰ προηγούμενα), which are "the duties of citizenship, marriage, begetting children, reverence to God, care of parents."[67] Indeed, for Epictetus, marriage is stripped of all the warmth one finds in Antipater, Hierocles, and Musonius. As we have noted, he says nothing of εὔνοια or of a husband and wife holding all things in common. Marriage is simply a civic duty.[68]

The Stoics, therefore, set their own mark upon the question whether one should marry. There were differences in emphasis and Epictetus could make exceptions for the Ideal Cynic. But the fundamental position is clear: marriage is desirable, for it sets a man free to pursue philosophy. And what is more, it is a duty one owes to the *polis*. For marriage is the only legitimate means of producing children and without children the cities and indeed the whole human race will not survive.

The appearance of the question whether marriage is desirable in rhetorical handbooks and in New Comedy demonstrates how it permeated society. The first century rhetorician Quintilian lists among the theses which "provide the most attractive and copious practice in the art of speaking" the title "Whether marriage is desirable" (*ducendane uxor*).[69] Three centuries later the question was still part of rhetorical education. Aphthonius gives an example of it in his *Progymnasmata*.[70] Moreover, this

---

[67] 3.7,25-26.

[68] In addition to 3.7 and 2.20, see *On the Faculty of Expression* (2.23,36-40) and *To Those Who Enter Light-Heartedly upon the Profession of Lecturing* (3.21,5-6). For Epictetus to say that the Cynic does not marry does not mean, however, that he neglects civic responsibilities. Indeed, the Cynic is involved in "exalted politics" (τηλικαύτη πολιτεία). There is no nobler office than his (3.22,83-85). Like Homer and the Theban general Epaminondas, the Cynic benefits society without producing children (3.22,77-81). His task, which he has been given by God, is "to oversee the rest of mankind," including those who have married and produced children. "Making his rounds like a physician, and feeling pulses," the Cynic determines, among other things, "who is treating his wife well and who ill" (3.22,72). Thus, the Cynic does not deny that marriage is a duty, but that it is *his* duty. Furthermore, Epictetus argues, the Cynic does in fact have children, since "[he] has made all mankind his children," reproving and chastening them not from idle impertinence, but as a father (3.22,81-82).

[69] *Institutio Oratoria* 2.4,24-25. See also 3.58. Text and translation in Loeb ed. Trans. Butler.

[70] For the text see Spengel 1854, vol 2, 50-53. An English translation is available in Nadeau 1952, 264-285.

44   Not like the Gentiles

example illustrates the impact of the Stoic view, for the issues it treats
are the very ones we have seen in the Stoic *topos On Marriage*.[71]
The weal and woe of married life was a frequent topic in New
Comedy.[72] But here, although many of the attitudes reflected in the
comedies echo the arguments of the *topos On Marriage*, the specifically
Stoic concern (the survival of the *polis*) is notably absent. For example,
Menander, who in fact was a student of Theophrastus,[73] has one of his
characters declare, "To have a wife and be the father of children, Parme-
non, entails many cares (μέριμνας) in life."[74] Menander, however, also
provides the opposite point of view. Another fragment reads, "If you come
to look at it, there's no such cosy combination, Laches, as is man and
wife."[75] One of the most interesting of the comedic treatments of marriage is from Menander's play, *The Misogynists*. Replying to Simylus's
disdain of marriage an unnamed character counters:

Yes, for you take it in left-handed style. That is you see in it
the difficulties (τὰ δυσχερᾶ) and that which annoys you (τὰ
λυπησαντά σε), but you have given up looking further at the
benefits (τὰ ἀγαθά). Now, Simylus, you'd not find a single one
of all your blessings with which there is not also combined
some evil. For instance, a wealthy wife is an irksome thing
(ὀχληρόν), nor does she even allow the one who took her to
wife to live as he likes. Yet there is a certain benefit accruing
from her, for example, children; or if her husband fall ill, she
nurses him carefully; she stays by him in adversity; she buries
him, if he die, and lays him out properly. Consider these points
whenever you are vexed by some everyday matter, for, if you
do you will put up with everything. Whereas if you are forever
picking out the annoying circumstances, without balancing

---

[71]For a list of parallels between the Stoic treatises and the
rhetoricians, see Praechter 1901,66-90 and 141-150. Praechter uses the
rhetoricians to support his reconstruction of the *topos On Marriage*, since
they show dependence on the Stoics in so many areas.
[72]Stobaeus cites the New Comedians (along with earlier comedians
such as Euripides) extensively.
[73]See Diog. Laer. *Lives* 5.36. For a discussion of the relationship
between Theophrastus and Menander on marriage, see Webster 1960, 214-
217.
[74]Stobaeus 4.517,9-10 Hense; in Körtes edition, frgm 647. The play is
unknown. Trans. Allinson. Loeb ed.
[75]Stobaeus 4.517,13-14 Hense; frgm 649K. The play is unknown. Trans.
Allinson. Loeb ed.

against them any of the things you may hope for, you will be forever tormented.[76]

This speech reflects the arguments of the philosophers at almost every point. The rhetoricians and comedians, therefore, doubtless played a large role in popularizing the ideas of the philosophers. Though at the same time, we must remember that the moral philosophers frequently did no more than reflect common notions of morality.

Finally, we must note that the question whether marriage is desirable was not simply an abstract one. We see this already in Antipater. He was concerned with "the weakness, anarchy, and inclination to sensual pleasure and the easy life" that obtained in many cities and contributed to a steadily declining birthrate among those with citizenship.[77] Two centuries later the emperor Augustus was plagued by the same problems. To combat them he enacted legislation that rewarded those who married and had three or more children while it punished those who had none.[78]

---

[76]Stobaeus begins the quotation with the words "a wealthy wife is an irksome thing . . ." (4.526,6 Hense; frgm 325K). Trans. Allinson. The speaker goes on to say that he will take his own daughter around the city to let prospective husbands see firsthand just what they are getting. This was very unusual in the Greek world, since women as a rule were confined to the women's quarters. See Dover 1974, 98.

[77]225,25-34 von Arnim. On the problems of low birthrates in Hellenistic cities, see Polybius Hist. 36.17, 5-10: "In our own time the whole of Greece has been subject to a low birth rate and a general decrease of population, owing to which cities have become deserted and the land has ceased to yield fruit, although there have neither been continuous wars nor epidemics . . . For as men had fallen into such a state of pretentiousness, avarice, and indolence that they did not wish to marry, or if they married, to rear children born to them, or at most as a rule but one or two of them, so as to leave these in affluence and bring them up to waste their substance, the evil rapidly and insensibly grew (Trans. Paton. Loeb ed.)." See further Balsdon 1969, 82-90.

[78]Augustus implemented two pieces of reform legislation dealing with marriage. The first was passed in 19/18 B.C.E. The legislation stipulated that all men between twenty-five and sixty and all women between twenty and fifty years of age should marry. It further imposed guidelines on marriage between social classes. Rewards were set for those who had three or more children and punishment for those who had none. The rewards entailed greater financial independence for mothers of three or more children and looser inheritance restrictions and more rapid career advancement for fathers. The punishment was severe tightening of inheri-

Interestingly, Dio Cassius attributes to Tiberius a speech given to the men of Rome when they were attempting to revoke Augustus's laws.[79] In this speech Tiberius rebukes those who refuse to marry and produce children, pointing out that for all they were doing the city of Rome was perishing. Moreover, the exhortations he gives them to marry suggest that his speechwriter could well have been a Stoic, for he refers to marriage as both a benefit and a civic obligation.[80] Clearly, therefore, the question whether marriage is desirable was a frequently debated one in Paul's world. When we turn to his treatment of marriage, we must examine the extent to which he reflects the arguments that were employed in the two sides of the debate.

WHOM ONE SHOULD MARRY

Many of those who advocated marriage went on to advise what kind of person one should marry and what kind one should avoid marrying. This advice, which with but rare exception was directed to men only, was even more formulaic in character than the discussion of whether one should

---

tance laws, so that bachelors and childless people were restricted in the amounts and sources of inheritance. The *lex Papia Poppaea* was passed in 9 C.E. It retained most of the restrictions, but did reflect a recognition that some people were quite unable to have children. On these laws, see Balsdon 1962, 75-79 and 89-90 and Corbett 1930, *passim*, but esp 119-121 and 133-135.

[79]See his *Roman History* 56.1-10. In an earlier speech Tiberius had praised those who had married and produced children. These, he observed bitterly, were far fewer than those who refrained from marrying.

[80]Tiberius argued that although there were disadvantages (δυσχερῆ) in marriage and having children, the advantages (τὰ ἀμείνονα) were more numerous (56.8,2-4). He had already listed these as a wife who is "chaste, a good housekeeper, a mother of children; one to gladden you in health, to tend you in sickness; to be your partner in good fortune, to console you in misfortune; to restrain the mad passion of youth and to temper the unseasonableness of old age," and children whom one leaves behind as successors and heirs (56.3,3-6). More important than these "private advantages" (τὰ κέρδη ἴδια), however, were the advantages deriving to the State. Primary among these was the very survival of Rome: Those who refused to marry and produce children, he charged, "are bent on destroying and bringing to an end the entire Roman nation" (56.4,4). Thus, to refrain from marrying and producing children was the worst of all possible crimes, worse even than murder (56.4,6). Trans. Cary. Loeb ed.

marry. For in almost all the philosophical treatises dealing with the selection of a wife, there is a warning against marrying for the sake of wealth, noble birth, and beauty, since those who married with these in mind obtained a tyrant and not a wife. Instead, one should look to the woman's character.

We have already seen this in Hierocles's treatise *On Marriage*. He had argued that marriage was a burden only to those who were foolish enough to marry for a large dowry or for beauty, since they were doomed to a life of struggle. He advises instead that one should be concerned with a woman's "character and way of life" (περὶ τῆς διαθέσεως καὶ τοῦ ἤθους).[81] Musonius treats this more fully, maintaining that her character (ψύχη) should possess "self-control" (σωφροσύνη), "justice" (δικαιοσύνη), and be "naturally disposed to virtue" (πρὸς ἀρετὴν εὐφυεστάτας).[82] He also adds to the warning against concern with genealogy, wealth, and beauty an exhortation to determine her bodily health and to learn whether she is capable of hard work and bearing children.[83] Antipater even advises on how one may determine a woman's character.[84] He should inquire into "the character and life-style of her parents" (τὸ τοῦ γονέως . . . . ἤθος καὶ τρόπον): The father should be "civic-minded" (πολιτικός), "refined" (ἄφορτος), "considerate" (εὐγνώμων), "temperate" (σώφρων), and "just" (δίκαιος).[85] The mother should have trained her daughter to emulate her way of life.[86] Furthermore, the parents should not have doted on the girl.[87] To learn these things, Antipater advises the prospective groom to make inquiries among the slaves and freedmen of the household, the neighbors, tradesmen, and the craftsmen and women who have access to the house, since they are in the best position to observe how the household is really run.[88]

---

[81]For Musonius's criticism of marrying for wealth, beauty, and noble birth, see *The Chief End of Marriage* B 90,8-11 Lutz. For Antipater on this, see 254,5-7 von Arnim.

[82]*The Chief End* B 90,4-13 Lutz.

[83]*The Chief End* B 90,8-11.

[84]*Concerning Life with a Woman* (περὶ γυναικὸς συμβιώσεως) 254,3-22 von Arnim.

[85]254,9-12.

[86]254,12-14.

[87]254,14-16.

[88]254,16-22. By contrast, see Ovid's advice on how to obtain a lover (including directions on where to go and how to act) in Book 1 of *The Art of Love*.

The Neo-Pythagoreans Pseudo-Occelus, Bryson, and Callicratidas share
the views of the Stoics regarding whom one should marry, though they
stress even more the dangers involved in marrying for wealth, beauty, and
noble birth.[89] Pseudo-Occelus, for example, argues that a man should
seek a woman "of comparable spirit and similar status" (συμπαθῆ τὴν
ψυχὴν καὶ ὁμοιοτάτην ἐπίδοξαν τῷ γένει),[90] since marriage with a rich
woman results in her ruling her husband, and that is "against the law of
nature" (παρὰ τὸν τῆς φυσέως νόμον).[91] Bryson adds to this the warning
that if a man marries simply for wealth, beauty, or social status, the
woman will soon cease to try to please her husband, since she will know
that he already has what he desires. She will then seek to control him, will
cease to work, and as a result the household will come to ruin.[92] Regarding the question of wealth, Callicratidas offers an admonition we have not
seen before. He warns not only against marrying a wealthy woman but
also against marrying below one's social status. For the one who marries
beneath himself, he argues, "subverts the dignity and splendor of the
family."[93] Thus, he advises, a man should choose a woman whose fortune
is conformable to his own.[94]

Another of the concerns the Neo-Pythagoreans raise is the question of
age. On the one hand this reflects their insistence that sexual intercourse
is for the sake of having children; on the other hand it reflects their fear

---

[89]For the text of Pseudo-Occelus On the Nature of the Universe, see
Thesleff 1965, 135-138. For his comments on marriage for beauty, wealth,
and noble birth, see 136, 15-16. (References to page and line of Thesleff.)
Bryson's Concerning Household Management survives only in Arabic and
Hebrew. These versions have been edited, with a German translation, by
Plessner (1928, 214-259). Thesleff (1965, 57-58) gives a brief synopsis in
English. For Bryson's views on beauty, wealth, and noble birth, see 2,85-88
(Plessner 237-238). For the text of Callicratidas's On the Happiness of
Households, see Thesleff 1965, 102-107. There is an English translation in
Taylor 1822, 50-57. For Callicratidas's comments on wealth, beauty, and
noble birth, see 106,14-18. (References to page and line of Thesleff.) For
the Neo-Pythagorean literature generally, see Thesleff 1961 and Städele
1980.
[90]136,19-20 Thesleff.
[91]136,24 Thesleff. Emphasis added. For Callicratidas, it is "unworthy
and unnatural" (ἀνάξιον καὶ παρὰ φύσιν) for a wife to rule her husband
(On the Happiness 106,19 Thesleff. Emphasis added.).
[92]Concerning Household Management 2.85 Plessner.
[93]Concerning Household Management 2,85 Plessner.
[94]On the Happiness 106,14-15.

of disturbing the natural order of husband and wife. Pseudo-Occelus, for example, argues repeatedly that the purpose of sexual intercourse is not pleasure but the birth of children (οὐχ ἡδονῆς ἕνεκα ἀλλὰ τέκνων γενέσεως).[95] Thus, he inveighs against those who marry a woman too old to bear children (ὑπερηλικεστέραν), rather than a woman able to bear a harvest of children.[96] And Callicratidas admonishes men to choose "a virgin in the flower of her youth. For such virgins are easily fashioned, and are docile; and are also naturally well disposed to be instructed by, and to fear and love their husbands."[97]

These arguments against marrying for wealth, beauty, and nobility were put to the challenge, however, in Plutarch's *Dialogue on Love*. The topic of the dialogue is whether homosexual or heterosexual love is better. In the course of the debate, the proponents of homosexual love take offense when a young man named Bacchon is pursued in marriage by a beautiful and wealthy widow several years older than he.[98] They warn that he should beware of her because "her determination [is] to command and to dominate [him]."[99] Their arguments were precisely those we have just noted in the Stoic and Neo-Pythagorean literature. Plutarch rejoins, however, that even "decent" (σώφρονες) women can be disagreeable and a poor woman can subject a man to her.[100] Thus, a woman's wealth by itself is not to be disdained. And, he adds, there have been men who married wealthy women without losing their dignity.[101] Therefore, "to choose a woman for her wealth rather than for her character of birth would be ignoble and base; but if character and good breeding are added, it would be ridiculous to shun her."[102] Moreover, age is no problem, Plutarch maintains, "as long as both parties are able to procreate."[103] And there is nothing dreadful about an older woman's being mistress of her younger husband, since one is, after all, always ruled by someone or something—whether it be a tutor, gymnasiarch, or the law itself. The older woman's superior intelligence makes her a fit mistress.[104]

---

[95]*On the Nature* 135,12-13, 14-15, 18-19 Thesleff.
[96]*On the Nature* 136,18-19.
[97]*On the Happiness* 107,7-11 Thesleff.
[98]*Dialogue* 2 (*Moralia* 749C-D). Trans Helmbold. Loeb ed.
[99]*Dialogue* 7 (*Moralia* 752E). Trans. Helmbold. Loeb ed.
[100]*Dialogue* 9 (*Moralia* 753C).
[101]*Dialogue* 9 (*Moralia* 753F-754A).
[102]*Dialogue* 9 (*Moralia* 754B-C).
[103]*Dialogue* 9 (*Moralia* 754B-C).
[104]*Dialogue* 9 (*Moralia* 754C-D).

Plutarch's rejoinder notwithstanding, the common view of the moralists was that a man should not marry for wealth, noble birth, or beauty. Instead he should marry a woman from his own social status, who is of good character, and who is young, healthy, and capable of bearing children.

Again, the comedians echo the arguments of the philosophers. The fragment from Menander's play *The Misogynists* quoted above refers to a wealthy wife as "an irksome thing"—for she does not allow her husband to live as he likes.[105] Anaxandrides repeats the warning that the man who marries a wealthy woman will not get a wife but a mistress.[106] One also finds in New Comedy, however, advice of a more substantive nature. Another of Menander's characters, for example, advises:

> We ought to do our marrying—yes, all of us by Zeus the saviour—as we do our shopping. We should not take scrutiny of useless details—"who was the grandfather of the girl one is to marry; who was her grandmother?"—while failing either to examine or observe the character (τρόπον) of the woman herself with whom one is to live.[107]

To be sure, the moralists' advice sometimes fell on deaf ears. Juvenal, for example, viciously satirizes men who marry for wealth and beauty.[108] And Augustus's legislation restricting inheritance confirms that fortune seeking was frequently a reason for marrying.[109] Indeed, even so staid a person as Pliny the Younger took note of wealth, looks, and genealogy when playing matchmaker for a friend's niece. In putting forward one of

---

[105]Stobaeus quotes Menander numerous times to this effect. See, for example, "To be rightly happy a man must needs inherit from his father. For the dower that enters the house with a wife is a possession that brings neither security nor charm" (4.519,24-520, 2 Hense; frgm 52K. Trans. Allinson. Loeb ed.); and "The man who would fain take to wife a wealthy hieress is either paying off some score of the gods' wrath or else he wishes to be luckless while hailed as a 'lucky man'" (4.458,8-10 Hense; frgm 585K. Trans. Allinson. Loeb ed.).

[106]Stobaeus 4.513, 7-9 Hense; frgm 52K.

[107]Stobaeus 4.513,7-9 Hense; frgm 52K.

[108]*Satire* 6,36-48.

[109]See n 78. MacMullen (1977, 190 n 38) points out that landholding records confirm that marriage was frequently a source of great wealth, since they reflect acquisitions of great estates through marriage. See also the literature he cites.

his own proteges, he describes him as having good looks of natural nobility, with the dignified bearing of a senator. Then he ponders whether he should also add that his father is of ample means since "the prevailing habits of the day and the laws of the country . . . judge a man's income to be of primary importance," concluding that because of children "the question of money must be taken into account as a factor influencing our choice."[110] Still, the values of the moralists do appear to have been held by many— even among those outside their ranks. Musonius and Pseudo-Occelus would doubtless have approved of Graxia Alexandria, whom her husband eulogized as "a woman of exemplary chastity who fed her sons at the breast."[111] And although Alciphron's *Letters of Fishermen* are an exercise in sophistry,[112] Panope's letter to Euthybolus doubtless reflects contemporary attitudes when in it Panope remonstrates her husband, "I was born of an honest father and an honest mother . . . and they gave me, formally betrothed and their sole heir, in wedlock to you for the begetting of legitimate children (ἐπὶ παίδων ἀροτῷ γνησίων).[113] Indeed, this last phrase was standard in Athenian[114] and Latin marriage contracts.[115] It is in funerary inscriptions, however, that one most readily finds corroboration for the wifely virtues listed by the moralists. The author of the so-called *Laudatio Turiae*,[116] for example, says of his wife

> Why should I mention your domestic virtues: your loyalty, obedience, affability, reasonableness, industry in working wool, religion without superstition, sobriety of attire, modesty of appearance.[117]

---

[110]*Letters* 1.14.9. Trans. Radice. Loeb ed.

[111]Dessau 1855, no 8451. Cited by Balsdon 1962, 201. See further, Aulus Gellius's account of Favorinus's encomium on breast feeding (*Attic Nights* 12.1).

[112]On Alciphron's *Letters*, see Jackson 1912, 67-96; Rohde 1914, 343-348; and Benner and Fobes's Introduction to the Loeb ed.

[113]1.6,1. Trans. Benner and Fobes, Loeb ed.

[114]See Aristaenetus 1.19 and Menander 435-436K.

[115]Two examples in Sanders 1938, 104-116. Sanders points out that the phrase in question (*liberorum procreandorum causa*) also occurs in Augustine's sermons 51.22 and 278.9.

[116]The identification of the author of the inscription as Q. Lucretius Vespillo and the woman as his wife Turia has been rejected by Durry 1950 and Wistrand 1976. Text, translation, and commentary in Wistrand 1976.

[117]"(30) *Domestica bona pudici[t]iae, opsequi, comitatis, facilitatis,*

Another Roman inscription reads:

> To a virtuous wife, and careful house-mistress, the desire
> of my soul, who has been with me eighteen years, three
> months and thirteen days. I have lived with her without one
> complaint . . .[118]

Even a slave could praise his wife for being "a good counsellor, prudent
and noble."[119]

To be sure, many of the phrases used in the inscriptions to praise a wife
became commonplace. To say that one's wife never caused one any grief,
for example, appears so frequently that it could simply be abbreviated
"s. u. q." (sine ulla querella).[120] But the frequency of the phrases demonstrates that they reflect society's ideals for wifely virtue.

There is, finally, one other criterion for choosing a wife which, because
of its rarity, deserves to be mentioned: the wife should share her husband's philosophical view of life. This was primarily a Cynic view. We
have already seen a hint of it in Epictetus's description of the Ideal Cynic.
He indicated that the Cynic missionary could marry only if he lived in a
city of wise men, since in this case both his wife and her relations would
be of the same persuasion as himself.[121] Epictetus cites as an example of
this kind of marriage Crates and Hipparchia.[122] In the later Cynic
Epistles, we find further evidence of this concern.[123] In the pseudony-
mous letters of Crates to Hipparchia,[124] for example, Hipparchia is

---

lanificii stud[i, religionis] (31) sine superstitione o[r]natus non con-
spiciendi, cultus modici cur [memorem? . . .]. Trans Wistrand. A less con-
spicuous inscription (Dessau 1855, no 8402) is dedicated to Amymone, "a
busy spinner, a good housewife, chaste, modest, and pius" (lanifica pia
pudica frugi casta domiseda). Trans. Friedländer 1913, vol 1, 264.

[118]Cited and translated by Friedländer 1913, vol 1, 264.

[119]Cited and translated by Friedländer 1913, vol 1, 266.

[120]See for example Dessau 1855, no 8156. "To the spirits of the
departed. To Cerellia Fortunata, dearest wife, with whom he lived forty
years without the slightest cause for complaint (s. u. g.), Marcus Antonius
Encolpus built this." Trans. Lewis and Reinhold 1955, vol 2, 285.

[121]3.22,68.

[122]3.22,76.

[123]On these epistles generally, see the introductions in Malherbe 1977a
and the bibliography given there.

[124]Text and translation (by Ronald F. Hock) in Malherbe 1977a. The
letters are attributed to Crates, but date from the first or second century

praised for having taken up the Cynic way of life with her husband and admonished not to relapse in her dedication to it by taking up such traditional wifely chores as spinning wool.[125] Crates reminds her that he did not marry her because he needed someone to take care of him by making tunics (which he could not wear anyway since Cynics are forbidden to wear such things) but because she yearned for philosophy.[126] Thus, he tells her "leave the wool-spinning, which is of little benefit, to the other women, who have aspired to none of the things you do"[127] and "try to be of greater benefit to human life."[128] This concern with sharing the philosophical way of life is especially striking since elsewhere the moralists' concern is only with the wife's sharing her husband's social status as defined by birth and wealth.

RELATIONS BETWEEN HUSBANDS AND WIVES

The moralists' concern with the relationship between husband and wife focused on two different issues: the special character of the relationship and the dominance of the husband. In a sense, of course, these two positions are contradictory, for although the moralists stress, for example, that husbands and wives share all things in common, they also maintain that it is the husband who rules. Moreover, although most of the moralists hold that the special character of the relationship between husbands and

---

C.E. See Hock's introduction to the letters of Crates in Malherbe 1977a, 10-13. References are to page and line of this collection.

[125] 82,6-7 Malherbe.

[126] 80,6-9. See also Diog. Laer. *Lives* 6.96, where Hipparchia argues with a certain Theodorus about her study of philosophy and rejection of the loom. Several of these letters argue for the equality of women. See, for example, Letter 28 ("Women are not by nature worse than men.") and Letter 23 ("Standfast, therefore, and live the Cynic life with us (for you are not by nature inferior to us), for female dogs are not by nature inferior to male dogs."). See also Letter 3 of Diogenes. But the attitude toward marriage is mixed. While Letters 28 and 31 of Crates refer to his marriage with Hipparchia, along with Letter 3 of Diogenes, Letter 47 of Diogenes explicitly forbids it: "One should not wed nor raise children, since our race is weak and marriage and children burden human weakness with troubles." Trans. Fiore. See also Letters 21, 42, and 44 of Diogenes, which reject all sexual intercourse with women.

[127] 82,9-11. Malherbe.

[128] 80,10-11 Malherbe.

wives demands that both be sexually faithful, others insist that the wife patiently bear her husband's infidelity.

The Peripatetic tradition maintained that a man should take care of his wife for the sake of the gods, "in whose presence he offered sacrifice and led his wife home, promising to honour her far above all others saving his parents." This meant that he remained faithful to her and "before all others loves and trusts her and holds her as his own."[129] Still, a woman comes to a man's house as a "suppliant."[130] The compiler of the Aristotelian *Magna Moralia* refers to a man's wife as "more nearly his equal" than other members of the household, so that "married life . . . is closely akin to the partnership between citizens." Nevertheless, he holds that "the wife is inferior to her husband."[131] Thus, the friendship that exists between them is "the friendship between unequals."[132] In practical terms, this meant for the Peripatetics that although both husband and wife were "contributing to the same end" (the well ordering of the household), "they are distinguished from each other by the possession of faculties not adapted in every case to the same tasks."[133] The determining factor here was that the man is stronger, the woman weaker. Thus, the man oversees affairs outside the household; the woman is mistress of affairs within the household.[134] Yet even where the wife is mistress, she must accede to her husband's wishes. For example, she must not allow anyone to enter the household without his knowledge. Indeed, her husband's customs (*viri mores*) are laws "appointed for her own life by divine will" (*a deo sibi impositas*). Only if he bids her do something base or unworthy of herself is she exempt from enduring all with patience and gentleness, even if his actions lead to the loss of his entire fortune.[135]

For the Neo-Pythagoreans the close relationship that exists between

---

[129]Pseudo-Aristotle, *Concerning Household Management* 3,2. Trans. Armstrong. Loeb ed.

[130]3.1 (*deprecator*). See also 1.4, where ἱκέτης is used.

[131]1.33.18.

[132]2.11,45 and 52.

[133]Pseudo-Aristotle, *Concerning Household Management* 1.3.

[134]1.3. This division of labor derives from Xenophon's *Concerning Household Management* and was presupposed by all the moralists except the authors of the Cynic epistles.

[135]Pseudo-Aristotle, *Concerning Household Management* 3.1. See also, the Letter of Melissa, according to which "the wishes of her husband ought to be an unwritten law to a well behaved wife" (*To Kleareta* 116,12-13 Thesleff. My translation.).

husbands and wives is part of the "divine order," which has determined that between them there is love and togetherness, making them as if they were one person.[136] But again the subservience of the woman is clearly expressed. To continue with Bryson: "It is the duty of the wife to acquiesce to her husband, to be subject to him, and to submit to what he demands of her, since he has bestowed his house upon her . . ."[137]

The contradiction between the special relationship between husbands and wives and the dominance of the husband is most acute, however, in Stoic literature—especially the diatribes of Musonius.[138] Musonius, as we have seen, spoke very highly of the relationship between husband and wife. He says, for example,

> In marriage there must be above all perfect companionship
> (πάντως συμβίωσις) and mutual love (κηδεμονίαν) of husband
> and wife, both in health and sickness and under all conditions,
> since it was with desire for this as well as having children
> that they both entered upon marriage. Where then this love
> for each other is perfect and they share it completely, each
> striving to outdo the other in devotion, the marriage is ideal
> and worthy of envy, for such a union is beautiful.[139]

And,

> To whom is everything judged to be common, body, soul, and
> possessions except man and wife? For these reasons all men

---

[136] *Concerning Household Management* 2.80-81 Plessner.

[137] 2.82 Plessner. For Callicratidas "wedlock is established with a view to the communion of life" (ἐπὶ βίου κοινωνία). Still, the husband is the ruler (ἄρχων), regulator (ἐπίτροπος), master (κυρίος), and praeceptor (ἐπιστάτης); the wife is the ruled (ἀρχόμενος), 107,4-5 Thesleff.

[138] The view expressed here is in agreement with Manning 1973, 72 and Balch 1981, Appendix 5, 143-149. Crouch 1972, 107 and Thraede 1977, 54-62 emphasize the distinctive character of the Stoic view. To be sure, the Stoic view, as seen for example in Musonius's claim that women too should study philosophy, is more liberal than that of the Neo-Pythagoreans and Peripatetics. But one cannot speak of "equality" between husbands and wives even in the Stoic position. For even Musonius, as we shall see, argues that the woman should be ready to serve her husband.

[139] *The Chief End* 88,17-23. Trans. Lutz.

consider the love of man and wife to be the highest form of love.[140]

Yet in spite of this "perfect companionship," "mutual love," and holding all things in common, and indeed, in spite of the fact that women too should study philosophy (since they have the same senses and the same parts of the body as men, as well as "a natural inclination toward virtue and the capacity for acquiring it"),[141] "even Musonius is still willing to employ the typical Greek distinctions between man and woman: stronger-weaker, ruler-ruled, better-worse."[142] Indeed, he even refers to the wife as a "great help" (μέγας ὄφελος) to her husband, adding that she must be willing "to serve [him] with her own hands (τῷ δὲ ἀνδρὶ ὑπηρετεῖν χερσὶ ταῖς ἑαυτῆς).[143] This last comment is only slightly less harsh than Antipater's claim that "the aim and goal of a woman's life" (σκόπον τοῦ βίου καὶ τέλος) should be to please (ἀρέσκειν) her husband.[144]

This ambiguity between the special relationship between husbands and wives and the dominance of the husbands obtains in the Middle-Platonic tradition also. Plutarch, for example, advises husbands to exercise control over their wives "not as the owner has control of property, but, as the soul controls the body, by entering into her feelings and being known to her through goodwill."[145] Nevertheless, most of the admonitions in his *Advice to Bride and Groom* are intended for wives, advising them to defer to their husband's wishes. For example:

---

[140] *Is Marriage a Handicap?* 94,8-11. Trans. Lutz.

[141] *That Women Too Should Study* 38,30-40,2.

[142] Balch 1981, 144.

[143] *That Women Too Should Study* 42,5-11. Trans. Lutz.

[144] 255,22-23 von Arnim. Antipater argued that husbands and wives should look at each other as the primary object of love (εὐνοίας), 255,11-12.

[145] *Advice to Bride and Groom* 33 (*Moralia* 142E). See also 34 (142F-143A), where Plutarch echoes the concern that husbands and wives share all things in common—bodies, property, friends, relations. He also speaks here of the importance of love (ἔρως) for the relationship between husband and wife: "the marriage of a couple in love with each other (ἐρώντων) is an intimate union (συμφυής); that of those who marry for dowry or children is of persons joined together (ἐκ συναπτομένων); and that of those who merely sleep in the same bed is of separate persons who may be regarded as cohabiting, but not really living together."

> Whenever two notes are sounded in accord, the true is carried
> by the bass; and in like manner every activity of a virtuous
> household is carried by both parties in agreement, but dis-
> closes the husband's leadership and preferences.[146]

One area in which the husband's preference is to be followed is in the
choice of friends: "A wife ought not to make friends of her own, but to
enjoy her husband's friends in common with him."[147] Interestingly, Plutarch interprets this to mean that the wife should also worship only her
husband's god, for

> The gods are the first and most important friends. Wherefore
> it is becoming for a wife to worship and to know only the gods
> that her husband believes in, and to shut the front door tight
> upon all queer rituals and outlandish superstitions, for with no
> god do stealthy and secret rites performed by a woman find
> favour.

Thus, Plutarch concludes that if women "subordinate (ὑποτάττουσαι)
themselves to their husbands, they are commended, but if they want to
have control, they cut a sorrier figure than the subjects of their control."[148]

As we saw above, for the Peripatetics the special nature of the relationship between husband and wife meant that the husband "before all
others loves and trusts [his wife] and holds her as his own."[149] For the
Peripatetics this meant paying to the wife the honors that are her due.
Primary among these is fidelity.

> Now to a wife nothing is of more value, nothing more right-
> fully her own, than honoured and faithful partnership with her
> husband. Wherefore it befits not a man of sound mind to
> bestow his person promiscuously, or have random intercourse
> with women; for otherwise the baseborn will share in the
> rights of his lawful children, and his wife will be robbed

---

[146] *Advice* 11 (*Moralia* 139D). Trans. Babbitt. Loeb ed.
[147] *Advice* 19 (*Moralia* 140D). Trans. Babbitt. Loeb ed.
[148] *Advice* 33 (*Moralia* 142E). Trans. Babbitt. Loeb ed.
[149] See above n 129.

(*privetur*) of her honour due, and shame be attached to his
sons.[150]

Musonius also denounces sexual intercourse outside of marriage, but he
is less concerned with its effect on the wife than with its effect on the
husband himself. Addressing those who claim that sexual intercourse with
a slave harms no one, he rejoins

> I continue to maintain that everyone who sins and does wrong
> (ἁμαρτάνει καὶ ἀδικεῖ), even if it affects none of the people
> about him, yet immediately reveals himself as a worse and
> less honourable person; for the wrong-doer by the very fact of
> doing wrong is worse and less honourable. Not to mention the
> injustice of the thing, there must be sheer wantonness in
> anyone yielding to the temptation of shameful pleasure and
> like swine rejoicing in his own vileness.[151]

Thus, he holds that sexual intercourse is justified only when it occurs in
marriage and for the sake of procreation.[152]

Plutarch, by contrast, is more ambiguous. While he advises the husband
that his conduct must be exemplary, since, as his wife's tutor in morals,
she is likely to imitate him,[153] his advice about sexual intercourse outside
of marriage is simply that a man should not resort to another woman
before having intercourse with his wife.[154] Moreover, to the wife he
advises that she should ask herself before seeking a divorce because of her
husband's infidelity, "Where else would my rival like better to see me,
what would she rather have me do, than feel aggrieved with my husband
and quarrel with him and abandon my very home and chamber?"[155]

The Neo-Pythagorean letters attributed to Theano, Euridice, and

---

[150]Pseudo-Aristotle, *Concerning Household Management* 3,2 (Trans.
Armstrong. Loeb ed.). See also, 1,3: "A man does wrong to his wife when
he associates with other women" (Trans. Armstrong. Loeb ed.).

[151]*On Sexual Indulgence* 86,24-29. Trans. Lutz.

[152]See, for example, in this same diatribe: "Men who are not wantons
or immoral are bound to consider sexual intercourse justified only when it
occurs in marriage and is indulged in for the purpose of begetting
children, since that is lawful, but unjust and unlawful when it is mere
pleasure-seeking, even in marriage" (86,4-8. Trans. Lutz).

[153]*Advice* 17 (*Moralia* 140C).

[154]*Advice* 44 (*Moralia* 144D).

[155]*Advice* 41 (*Moralia* 140A).

Nicostrata offer similar counsel to the woman whose husband consorts with courtesans.[156] She should bear it patiently and by her conduct seek to bring about a reconciliation with him, recognizing that he sees a courtesan simply for pleasure while his relations with her are guided by reason.[157] The worst that these letters say about a man's infidelity is that it is "madness" (παράνοια) and a "disease" (νόσος).[158]

Again, the evidence demonstrates that the views of the moralists were shared by people outside philosophical circles. We have already seen that the funerary inscriptions praised women for their chastity, loyalty, obedience, and domestic skills. The Greek marriage contracts of Egypt regularly contain clauses stipulating that the husband must provide for his wife in a manner suitable to her status and not have children by another woman while she is alive, upon pain of forfeiting her dowry.[159] There are likewise clauses specifying that the wife should not stay the night away from her home without her husband's consent, should not consort with another man, or do anything to dishonor her husband, again upon pain of forfeiting her dowry.[160]

Guarding one's chastity and remaining faithful to one's spouse is also

---

[156]On these letters see Thesleff 1961.

[157]To Euridice 197,12-24 Thesleff.

[158]To Nicostrata 198,30 and 32 Thesleff.

[159]See, for example, P. Teub. 104 (92 B.C.E.), "It shall not be lawful for Philiscus to bring in another wife besides Apollonia, nor to keep a concubine or boy, nor to have children by another woman while Apollonia lives, nor to inhabit another house over which Apollonia is not mistress, nor to eject or insult or ill-treat her, nor to alienate any of their property to the detriment of Apollonia. If he is proved to be doing any of these things or fails to supply her with necessaries or clothing or other things as stated, Philiscus shall forthwith forfeit to Apollonia the dowry of 2 talents 4000 drachmae of copper." A similar, less specific phrase occurs in P. Ryl. 154 (66 C.E.) and P. Oxy. 1273 (260 C.E.): "Let them [sc. the married couple] live together blamelessly" (συμβιούτωσαν οὖν ἀλλήλοις . . . ἀμέμπτως). These three manuscripts are readily available in Select Papyri vol 1 of the Loeb ed. Trans. Hunt and Edgar.

[160]P. Teub. 104, again, "It shall not be lawful for Apollonia to spend the night or day away from the house of Philiscus without Philiscus's consent or to consort with another man or to dishonor the common home or to cause Philiscus to be ashamed by any act that brings shame upon a husband" (Trans. Hunt and Edgar, Loeb ed.). For a discussion of the legal status of the various forms of Hellenistic marriage contracts, with further examples, see Wolff 1939.

the theme of the Greek romance. The plot of these early novels involves the sudden, forced separation of a couple recently, or about to be, married and their efforts to remain faithful to one another in the midst of various adventures. In Xenophon of Ephesus's *Ephesiaca,* for example, the newly married Habrocomes and Anthea make a vow to face death rather than be unfaithful to one another. Almost immediately they are separated because of Cupid's jealousy of Habrocomes's beauty and first one and then the other fall into situations in which their vow is put to the test. Habrocomes is pursued by both men and women; and Anthea is threatened with assault by robbers and those who have bought her. Indeed, she even marries twice, though by appealing to one husband and tricking another she manages to avoid consummating the unions. In the end, of course, they are reunited. Anthea can then tell Habrocomes that she has kept her vow, in spite of many suitors and forceful attacks upon her. And Habrocomes replies that he, too, has been faithful and remains as pure as when she last saw him.[161] To be sure, Habrocomes's disclaimer is not quite true. He in fact succumbed to one of his temptresses. But even this allowance for the husband fits with what we have seen in some of the moralists.

THE SIGNIFICANCE OF PRODUCING CHILDREN

As we saw in the survey of the question whether marriage is desirable, producing children was given as one of the primary reasons for marrying. Since we gave examples of this argument there, it is necessary here only to summarize the evidence.

In the first place, it was argued that children are "beneficial" in that they are help to parents who are still working and succor to parents who are aged and infirm. Next, they are the means whereby the survival of the human race and the continued worship of the gods are assured. But most important, especially for the Stoics, children are the means whereby the city is to survive. Thus, producing children became a civic duty. Indeed, Musonius could argue that since lawgivers forbade abortion, discouraged childlessness, rewarded large families, and punished those without children, one cannot avoid doing wrong by failing to do what the lawgivers decree.[162]

---

[161]Xenophon of Ephesus 5.14,2-4 (Papanikalaou 1973, 70). An English translation is available (along with Longus's *Daphnis and Chloe* and Dio Chrysostom's "The Hunters of Euboea" from the *Seventh Discourse)* in Hadas 1964, 71-126.

[162]*Should Every Child that is Born be Raised?* 96,12-25 Lutz.

Here again, the evidence suggests that having children was a goal for many outside philosophical circles. As we have seen, Augustus's legislation encouraged having more than three children.[163] Later emperors would even provide child support, so that poverty could not be used as an excuse not to have children, or to expose them once they were born.[164] The *Laudatio Turiae* illustrates the lengths some would consider in order to have children. The wife eulogized in this inscription offered to divorce her husband and procure for him another wife who was able to bear children so that he might obtain an heir.[165]

To be sure, abortion and, especially among the poor, the exposing of children were common.[166] But the large numbers of people living in even small houses in rural Egypt suggest that having many children was a common goal. One census report records that in a single house lived a husband and wife with their six children, two daughters-in-law with their three children, a sister-in-law with her two children, a tenant and his wife with their child, along with other in-laws: a total of twenty-four persons,

---

[163]See above n 78. In certain circumstances, one could be exempt from this law. Yet even among those who were exempt, some, such as Pliny the Younger, still desired to have children. Upon receipt of the privilege, he writes Trajan to express his gratitude, adding, "Still more now do I long for children of my own, though I wanted them even during those evil days now past, as you may know from my being married twice . . . Now is the time I would wish to be a father, when my happiness need know no fear" (*Letters* 10.2.2-3. Trans. Radice. Loeb ed.). Trajan's response to Pliny's letter requesting the privilege for Suetonius Tranquillus illustrates how reluctant emperors were to grant the exemption (10,95).

Augustus's legislation was directed to the citizen class. Columella states in his treatise On *Agriculture* (1,6) that he extended privileges to female slaves who bore many children also: "A mother of three children received exemption from work, a mother of more, her freedom as well."

[164]On this see Balsdon 1969, 88-90 and the literature cited there.

[165]2,25-50. Petronius's hero Trimalchio also refuses to dismiss his wife because they have no children (*Satyricon* 74). By contrast, the first divorce in the Roman Republic was said to have been caused by a wife's sterility. See Valerius Maximus 2.1,4.

[166]On abortion, see Pomeroy 1965, 166-168 and the literature cited there. P. Oxy. 744 is frequently cited with regard to exposing children. In this letter, a husband directs his wife, "If by chance you bear a child, if it is a boy, let it be, if it is a girl, cast it out." The letter is readily available in *Select Papyri* vol 1, 294-295 Loeb ed. Trans. Hunt and Edgar. See further Balsdon 1962, 193 and 196-197.

half of whom were children.[167] And indeed, many of the children who had been exposed were rescued and raised by others. B.G.U. 1107 (13 B.C.E.), for example, tells of one Isidora who took pity on an exposed child and obtained a nurse for it. P. Oxy. 37 (49 C.E.) relates the fate of another child who was "picked up from the garbage dump" (ἀνεῖλεν ἀπὸ κοπρίας). Having been found and entrusted to a nurse, it became the subject of a legal dispute between the finder and the woman who had been engaged to nurse it. The nurse had kidnapped the child, claiming it as her own.[168] Funerary inscriptions, moreover, demonstrate that the death of a child was keenly felt by its parents. In one of many such inscriptions, the parents of a girl who had lived one year, eleven months, and three days mourn her premature death (defuncto acervo), describing her as "the sweetest of spirits" (spirito dulcissimo), and themselves as "sad and most unhappy" (acervi et infelicissimi).[169] Another set of parents erect a monument to their son Eucopion who had lived only six months and three days, "the sweetest and dearest infant who, although not yet able to speak, was the most delightful thing" (infanti dulcissimo suavissimoque, qui cum nondum fari potuisset iucundissimo).[170] Such expressions of tenderness, not to mention pain, demonstrate that children were valued not simply by the moralists who were concerned with the survival of the state, but also by common people with little appreciation of the nuances of moral philosophy.

---

[167]B.G.U. 115. Cited by MacMullen 1974, 13.

[168]To be sure, many of those who found exposed children rescued them only to keep or sell them as slaves. As MacMullen (1974, 14) observes, "nothing was wasted in the ancient world: not an abandoned baby, not the cloth that kept the ragpicker in business, not the empty fisherman's shack on the beach, not even the grains of barley in horse manure in the streets." Still, funerary inscriptions dedicated by foundlings to those who had rescued them suggest that exposed children sometimes had a good life. They refer to their rescuers as their "educator, nutritror, or patronus (or patrona) recording gratitude for kindness received ('patrono benignissimo', 'patronae benignissimae') ... in language of warm affection." (Balsdon 1969, 87 with references and further literature). The pastoral romance Daphnis and Chloe reflects the close relationship that could develop between a foundling and its adopted parents.

[169]Dessau 1855, no 8486. My trans.

[170]Dessau 1855, no 8487. My trans.

CONCLUSIONS

There is, of course, much more that one can say about sexual morality in Greco-Roman society. Doubtless, there was a great deal of immorality. We have mentioned in passing that abortion and the exposure of children were common. Prostitution and the keeping of courtesans were equally common, as was the employment of slaves to satisfy one's sexual desires.[171] We have also noted that many married simply to have access to a large fortune. Divorce too was exceedingly frequent. Seneca, for example, ridicules some women for marking the years not by the changing of censors but by the acquisition of a new husband.[172] A more prosaic comment comes from the inscription dedicated to "Turia": "Marriages as long as ours are rare, marriages that are ended by death and not broken by divorce."[173] Such comments reveal that many did not value marriage very highly.

Our purpose here, however, has not been to describe sexual morality in the Greco-Roman world, but to examine what it was people actually said when they gave advice on marriage and to determine the extent to which the values expressed in this advice may have been shared by others. We can only conclude from what we have seen that for many marriage and the stability of the home was indeed very important. We must, therefore, take this into account when we examine Paul's advice on marriage to the Thessalonians and Corinthians.

---

[171]See, for example, Carcopino 1940, 95-100; Friedländer 1907, 215-219 and 241-261. Hock 1982 gives an extensive list of texts dealing with prostitution and courtesans.

[172]On Benefits 3.16,2. See also Juvenal Satire 6.224-230.

[173]Laudatio Turiae 1.27.

3

The Precepts on Marriage and
Sexual Morality in 1 Thess 4:3-8

Within months of completing his mission in Thessalonica Paul wrote a letter to the church in that city encouraging them in their new faith.[1] It is in this letter that Paul's earliest reference to marriage and sexual morality occurs. In 1 Thess 4:3-8 he cites three specific precepts:

(1) ἀπέχεσθαι ἀπὸ τῆς πορνείας (v 3b),

(2) εἰδέναι ἕκαστον ὑμῶν τὸ ἑαυτοῦ σκεῦος κτᾶσθαι ἐν ἁγιασμῷ καὶ τιμῇ (v 4),

(3) τὸ μὴ ὑπερβαίνειν καὶ πλεονεκτεῖν ἐν τῷ πράγματι τὸν ἀδελφὸν αὐτοῦ (v 6a)

These precepts were not new to the Thessalonians. They were part of the paraenetic tradition Paul had delivered to them during his founding mission.[2] Here in the letter, therefore, Paul simply *reminds* the Thessalo-

---

[1]General scholarly opinion holds that Paul, along with Timothy and Silvanus, founded the church in Thessalonica on the so-called second missionary journey in 49 and that 1 Thessalonians was written during the early stages of his mission in Corinth, which lasted from January 50 to mid 51. This makes 1 Thessalonians the earliest of Paul's letters. For a discussion of the evidence, see the commentaries and Kümmel 1975, 257-260.

[2]Note "as you received from us" (καθὼς παρελάβετε παρ᾽ ἡμῶν, v 1); "for you know what precepts we gave to you" (οἴδατε γὰρ τίνας παραγγελίας ἐδώκαμεν ὑμῖν, v 2); "as indeed we told you before and solemnly warned you" (καθὼς καὶ προείπαμεν ὑμῖν καὶ διεμαρτυράμεθα, v 6); and "as we instructed you" (καθὼς ὑμῖν παρηγγείλαμεν, v 11).

nians of his earlier teaching. Why? Some scholars suggest that when Timothy returned to Paul with his report that the Thessalonians remained faithful to the gospel and continued to hold Paul in fond memory (3:6-10), he also brought news that some of them had fallen into the immoral practices associated with their former worship of idols.[3] Others maintain that Paul *feared* the Thessalonians might revert to the immorality of their former life, since they had only recently turned from idols to serve God.[4] Still other scholars claim that Timothy brought with him specific questions about marriage and sexual morality which had arisen among the Thessalonians after Paul had left and about which they wanted Paul's counsel.[5] And still others argue that there was nothing in Thessalonica prompting Paul to rehearse the precepts on marriage and sexual morality, that he did so as a matter of course—simply because these were common themes in the moral literature of the time and like other moralists he addresses them when summarizing his ethical teaching.[6]

None of these answers is adequate. There is no evidence that the Thessalonians were living immorally or were in danger of doing so. On the contrary, Timothy gave them a good report (3:6). Similarly, there is no indication that Paul was answering questions in vv 3-8. He was reminding the Thessalonians of what they already knew. And while it is certainly true, as we have seen in the two preceding chapters, that concern with marriage and sexual morality was common for the Hellenistic moralists and for Jewish paraenetic traditions, and that precepts addressing both topics were frequently included in ethical summaries—to say this alone does not adequately explain how and why Paul refers to them in this letter. For it ignores the emphasis Paul places on the precepts dealing with marriage and sexual morality and overlooks their significance for the Thessalonian community.

---

[3] Jewett 1971, 109.
[4] This is the most common explanation. See, for example, Dibelius 1937, 20, Rigaux 1956, 502, Best 1972, 159-160. A variation of this is Dobschütz's suggestion that Paul was reacting to problems in Corinth, from which 1 Thessalonians was written (1909, 169).
[5] Best 1972, 154 and 162; Faw 1952, 217-225.
[6] Dibelius 1937, 19. See also the treatment of the nature of paraenesis in his commentary on James (1976, 1-11). Ronald Hock (1982, 54) argues that Paul "like his contemporaries in the Greek East, could not avoid the subject [of sexual morality], given the pervasiveness of the world of love in social experience and the vital role this world had assumed in intellectual life."

The importance of these precepts for Paul and for the Thessalonians is reflected in the claims Paul makes about them. These claims, which comprise more than half of this section (vv 3a, 5, and 6b-8), remind the Thessalonians that living by the precepts on marriage and sexual morality attunes them to the will of God, distinguishes them from the surrounding world, and insures good order within the family of God. Thus, it is not the precepts themselves but the claims made about them which provide the real clues for understanding why Paul refers to marriage when writing to the Thessalonians.

But before analysing Paul's formulation of the precepts on marriage and sexual morality, it is important to note that vv 3-8 comprise only one segment of a larger unit—4:1-12. An *inclusio* formed by περιπατεῖν ("to live," literally, "to walk"), in vv 1 and 12 marks 4:1-12 as the first unit within the section of the letter introduced by the transitional λοιπὸν οὖν ἀδελφοί. Thus, the precepts Paul cites in vv 1-12 demonstrate for the Thessalonians "how [they] should *live* in order to please God" (τὸ πῶς δεῖ [αὐτοὺς] περιπατεῖν καὶ ἀρέσκειν θεῷ) and how they must conduct themselves in order to "*live* in a seemly manner before outsiders and be in need of nothing" (περιπατεῖν εὐσχημόνως πρὸς τοὺς ἔξω καὶ μηδενὸς χρείαν ἔχειν).

Within this *inclusio* there are seven specific precepts dealing with day-to-day life. Vv 3-8 contain the first three, the precepts on marriage and sexual morality. The precepts of the second segment (vv 9-12, set off by the introductory περι δε) are less homogeneous. The first concerns "brotherly love" (φιλαδελφία). Paul asserts that there is no need for him to give the Thessalonians any guidance concerning this issue because they themselves are "taught by God ... to love one another" (θεοδίδακτοι . . . εἰς τὸ ἀγαπᾶν ἀλλήλους), which they are already doing not only to one another but also "to all the brothers in the whole of Macedonia" (vv 9-10).

The last three precepts are distinct from the precept on "brotherly love" but are related to one another. They exhort the Thessalonians "to live quietly and to mind their own affairs and to work with their own hands" (ἡσυχάζειν καὶ πράσσειν τὰ ἴδια καὶ ἐργάζειν ταῖς ἰδίαις χερσὶν ὑμῶν, v 11). Although Paul makes no explicit theological justification for these last three precepts as he did for the others, he does add to them the concluding ἵνα clause, "so that you may live seemly before outsiders and be in need of nothing."

To be sure, the precepts in vv 9-12 are materially distinct from those in vv 3-8 and formally separated from them by περι δε in v 9. Nevertheless, because they are all concerned with how believers should "live," we must take them into account as we analyze the formulation and function of the precepts on marriage and sexual morality. Moreover, just as we must focus on the claims Paul makes about the precepts in vv 3-8, so we must examine the claims he makes about those in vv 9-12.

TRANSLATING THE PRECEPTS IN 1 THESS 4:3-8

Translating 1 Thess 4:3-8 is notoriously difficult. Althought the first of the precepts is straightforward—"Abstain from sexual immorality"—the others are fraught with problems. In the second precept the most difficult problem is the phrase ἑαυτοῦ σκεῦος κτᾶσθαι. The language is clearly metaphorical. But to what does it refer? Recent translations render it in three different ways:

(1) "to take a wife for himself" (RSV);
(2) "to gain mastery over his body" (NEB);
(3) "[to guard] his member" (NAB).

The evidence is ambiguous at every point, as the translations suggest. In the present tense, which occurs here, κτᾶσθαι normally means "acquire" or "purchase." But scholars who translate along the lines of the NEB or NAB point out that on occasion the present tense of κτᾶσθαι took on the meaning of the perfect tense and thus could be rendered "to possess," "to keep," "to guard," or even "to gain mastery over."[7]

Similarly, there is evidence to support all three readings of σκεῦος. In a number of Rabbinic sayings כלי is used metaphorically for a woman; in later Greco-Roman thought the body was described as a "vessel" for the soul, a metaphor some scholars find in Rom 9:22-23 and 2 Cor 4:7; and in 1 Sam 21:6 of the MT the male sexual organ is referred to as a כלי— "vessel," "weapon," or "tool."[8]

Moreover, as the commentaries show, all three translations can be made to fit the context. Thus, one may agree with Ernest Best who

---

[7] For the evidence from the papyri, see Moulton-Milligan 1930, 361-362.

[8] Scholars who interpret σκεῦος as "body" include: Rigaux (1956, 504-506), Milligan (1908, 48-49), Preisker (1927, 127, n 72), and Dibelius (1937, 21). Those who prefer "wife" include: Dobschütz (1909, 163-165), Frame (1912, 149-150), Ellicott (1884, 63-65), Maurer (1971, 365-367), Best (1972, 162), Klassen (1978, 166-167), Hock (1982, 40-43), and Meeks (1983, 228 n 130). The most comprehensive treatment of σκεῦος as the male sexual organ is Whitten 1982, 142-143.

observes that there is nothing which forbids any of these readings and a great deal which encourages them.⁹ The strongest case, however, can be made in favor of translating ἑαυτοῦ σκεῦος κτᾶσθαι as "obtain a wife." The most telling argument for this reading is 1 Cor 7:2, for here Paul's advice on marrying is formally the same as that in 1 Thess 4:3b-4, but in less metaphorical language.¹⁰ Like 1 Thess 4:3b-4, 1 Cor 7:2 begins with a reference to sexual immorality: διὰ δὲ τὰς πορνείας. Then Paul charges, "Let each man have his own wife and let each woman have her own husband." The rule, of course, is developed beyond what one finds in 1 Thess 4:4, for here it advises women as well as men.¹¹ Nevertheless, the first part of the rule is exactly the same, except in more direct speech:

εἰδέναι ἕκαστον ὑμῶν τὸ   ἑαυτοῦ σκεῦος κτᾶσθαι
ἕκαστος   τὴν ἑαυτοῦ γυναῖκα ἐχέτω.

To press this argument further, Paul's formulation of the precepts in 1 Thess 4:3b-4 and 1 Cor 7:2 is strikingly similar to two precepts we noted in the survey of Jewish paraenetic teaching on marriage: Tob 4:12 and T. Levi 9:9-10. Both of these precepts begin with a warning against sexual immorality and then, like 1 Cor 7:2, advise marriage in explicit language.

πρόσεχε, τεκνόν, ἀπὸ τοῦ πνεύματος τῆς πορνείας· τοῦτο γὰρ ἐνδελεχεῖ καὶ μέλλει διὰ τοῦ σπέρματός σου μιαίνειν τὰ ἅγια. λάβε οὖν σεαυτῷ γυναῖκα, ἔτι νέος ὢν μὴ ἔχουσαν μῶμον μηδὲ βεβηλωμένην μηδὲ ἀπὸ γένους ἀλλοφύλων ἢ ἐθνῶν (T. Levi 9:9-10).¹²

πρόσεχε σεαυτῷ, παιδίον, ἀπὸ πάσης πορνείας καὶ γυναῖκα πρῶτον λαβὲ ἀπὸ τοῦ σπέρματος τῶν πατέρων σου· μὴ λάβῃς γυναῖκα ἀλλοτρίαν ἢ οὐκ ἔστιν ἐκ τῆς φυλῆς τοῦ πατρός σου, διότι υἱοὶ προφητῶν ἐσμέν (Tob 4:12).

The formal similarities are clear. Furthermore, one finds here the same concern with "holiness" and the dangers inherent in sexual conduct of "outsiders" that one finds in 1 Thess 4:3b-5 and 1 Cor 7:2. Thus, Tob 4:12

⁹Best 1972, 161. He refers specifically to the interpretations of σκεῦος as "body" and "wife."
¹⁰This has been noted by Lightfoot (1895, 55), Best (1972, 162), Klassen (1978, 167), Hock (1982, 41) and Meeks (1983, 228 n 130).
¹¹We will examine 1 Cor 7:2 further in the following chapter.
¹²The Greek text is taken from de Jonge 1978, 36.

and *T. Levi* 9:9-10 suggest that the precepts Paul cites in 1 Thess 4:3b-5 are based on traditional precepts of Jewish paraenesis which couple warnings against sexual immorality with advice on obtaining a wife and that consequently ἑαυτοῦ σκεῦος κτᾶσθαι should be translated "obtain a wife."

A fresh look at the linguistic evidence confirms this reading of 1 Thess 4:3b-4. (1) To speak of "obtaining" a wife was in fact a common idiom in both Hebrew and Greek usage, reflecting the view of both cultures that the wife passed into her husband's possession at marriage.[13] Christian Maurer overlooks this in his influential article on σκεῦος in the TDNT.[14] Maurer attempted to resolve the dilemma of σκεῦος κτᾶσθαι by seeking to relate the phrase "to the larger linguistic context and to consider the reciprocal interaction between Greek and Hebrew usage."[15] This approach is correct. But there are problems with his reading of the evidence.

Maurer argues that σκεῦος κτᾶσθαι is Paul's rendering of two Hebrew phrases: בעל אשה ("to possess a woman sexually") and שמש כלי ("to use as a vessel"). He points out that בעל can be taken ingressively ("to become lord and master in marriage") or duratively ("to be a husband"). Although Maurer recognizes that συνοικεῖν (or συνοικίζειν) is used to translate בעל in all of his examples of בעל אשה, he nevertheless claims that Paul used κτᾶσθαι since, "in the Jewish sphere, under the influence of the similar development of בעל, κτᾶσθαι comes to have a stronger durative sense."[16] The evidence, however, does not bear out this claim. In the first instance, Maurer does not demonstrate that בעל underwent a change in meaning, for the rabbinic evidence he cites reflects continued use of both the ingressive and durative senses of the word. Second, the three references for the durative use of κτᾶσθαι (none of which refers to obtaining or possessing a wife) are not enough to demonstrate a shift in emphasis, for, as Maurer himself notes, κτᾶσθαι also continues to be used in the ingressive sense.

Furthermore, in seeking to establish the durative sense of κτᾶσθαι, Maurer has slighted more relevant evidence. For in Ruth 4:10 and Sir

---

[13]To be sure, the legal status of women was undergoing significant change in the early years of the Roman Empire. See Pomeroy 1975, chapter 8 and Meeks 1983, 23-25. The traditional language, however, continued to be used.

[14]1971, 358-367.

[15]365.

[16]366. On the ingressive use of κτᾶσθαι he points to Sir. 36:24 and Ruth 4:10, which we will look at below.

36:24 κτᾶσθαι occurs with the sense of "to acquire" a wife. And in both instances it translates קנה and not בעל:

את-רות . . . קניתי לי לאשה.
Ρουθ . . . κέκτημαι ἐμαυτῷ εἰς γυναῖκα.
(Ruth 4:10)

קנה אשה ראשית קנין.
ὁ κτώμενος γυναῖκα ἐνάρχεται κτήσεως.
(Sir 36:24(25))[17]

This use of קנה becomes fixed in rabbinic literature where it is a technical term for "acquiring a woman in marriage."[18] For example, Qiddušin, the tractate of the Mishnah and Talmud dealing with the laws of betrothal and marriage, opens with the saying, "By three means is the woman acquired (האשה נקנית) and by two means she acquires her freedom. She is acquired by money or by writ or by intercourse" (m. Qidd. 1:1).[19]

Therefore, since συνοικεῖν was used to translate בעל and since κτᾶσθαι was used to render קנה, it seems much more likely that קנה אשה is the Hebrew equivalent of σκεῦος κτᾶσθαι and not בעל אשה This would mean, of course, that it should be translated "obtain a wife" and not "possess a wife."

Furthermore, as suggested above, to speak of "obtaining" a wife was not simply Hebrew idiom. Although γαμεῖν ("to marry"), λαμβάνειν (εἰς) γυναῖκα ("To take (for) a wife"), and ἔχειν (εἰς) γυναῖκα ("to have (for) a wife") were the more common Greek expressions, γυναῖκα κτᾶσθαι was also current. Two examples will suffice to demonstrate this. In his Symposium Xenophon has Socrates respond to those who questioned his marriage to Xanthippe (who had the reputation of being a shrew), "I have got her (ταύτην κέκτημαι) well assured that if I can endure her, I shall have no difficulty in my relations with the rest of human kind."[20] And the Collectio Vindobonensis attributes to the sage Cleoboulos the admonition "Marry (γάμει) someone like yourself, for if you marry (γάμῃς) someone superior to yourself, you will obtain (κυήσῃ) a ruler and not a partner."[21]

---

[17]The Hebrew text of Sirach is taken from Segal 1959, 229 [רכט].
[18]See Jastrow 1967, 1391.
[19]Trans. Danby. See also b. Ketub. 82b and Qidd. 7a.
[20]2:10. Loeb ed. Trans. Todd.
[21]Lesky (1966, 155) dates this collection to the sixth century, but it

The evidence, therefore, is clear: to speak of "obtaining a wife" was standard usage. The fact remains, however, that in 1 Thess 4:3b-4 Paul did not write γυναῖκα κτᾶσθαι but σκεῦος κτᾶσθαι

(2) Maurer cited a number of rabbinic passages to establish the metaphorical use of כלי to describe a woman. Again, however, there is a problem with his evidence in that all the sayings he cites are late.[22] This means, of course, that one cannot legitimately claim that Paul was influenced by them. If, however, one looks beyond the single Hebrew term כלי to other words and phrases which refer to a woman as some kind of vessel, one discovers how common the metaphor in fact was and how early it appears.

Prov 5:15-18, for example, uses several different terms to refer to a woman as a container of water, with clear sexual overtones:

Drink water from your own cistern (בור; LXX ἀγγεῖον);
Flowing water from your own well (באר; LXX φρέαρ πηγῆς).
Should your springs (עין; LXX τὰ ὕδατα ἐκ τῆς σῆς πηγῆς)
    be scattered abroad,
Streams of water (פלגי-מים; LXX τὰ ὕδατα) in the street?
Let your fountain (מקור; LXX ἡ πηγὴ τοῦ ὕδατος) be blessed,
And rejoice in the wife of your youth.

M. Ketub. 3:4-5 refers to a woman as an "earthen pot" (עציץ). This passage is especially important because it is earlier than the rabbinic references cited by Maurer and others and because it refers to a woman as a vessel in the context of discussion of marriage law:

Wherein does the violator differ from the seducer? The violator pays [compensation for] the pain and the seducer does not pay [compensation for] the pain; the violator must pay forthwith, but the seducer only if he puts her away; the violator *must drink out of his own earthen pot* (עציץ), but if the seducer is minded to put her away he may put her away. How does he "drink out of his earthen pot"? [He must marry her] even if she was lame, even if she was blind, and even if she was afflicted with boils. But if she was found unchaste or was not fit to be taken in marriage by an Israelite he may not

----

contains much older traditions. The relevant section on "The Sayings of the Seven Sages" may be found in the Gaisford edition of Stobaeus vol 4., p. 960. The translation here is my own.
[22]He cites *b. Meg.* 12b, *B. Mes.* 84b, and *Sanh.* 22b.

continue [his union] with her, for it is written, And she shall be to him for a wife—a wife that is fit for him. (Emphasis added)[23]

Three other sayings from rabbinic literature should be mentioned here, for they demonstrate how many different terms were used. *B. Ned.* 20b attributes to Rab the saying: "One may not drink out of one goblet (זה כוס) and think of another (כוס אחר)." The rabbis interpret this to mean that a man should not think of another woman when engaged in sexual intercourse. According to *b. Pesaḥ* 112a-b, R. Akiba says to R. Simeon b. Yoḥai, "Do not cook in a pot (קדירה) in which your neighbor has cooked." Again the rabbis interpret: "What does this mean? [Do not marry] a divorced woman during her husband's lifetime." And finally *b. Sanh.* 152a records an anonymous saying in which a woman is described as "a pitcher (חמה) full of filth with its mouth full of blood."[24]

These examples show that many different terms were used to describe a woman as a vessel. The broad range of terms, the different traditions in which they occur, and the early date for some of them suggest that the metaphorical use of כלי and other related terms was common in Hebrew usage and already established in Paul's time. Thus, the tradition Paul quotes in 1 Thess 4:4 is in keeping with the metaphorical use of כוס, כלי, עצץ, etc., when it refers to a woman as a σκεῦος.[25]

The third precept raises another set of problems. Many scholars argue that Paul shifts to another topic here—business.[26] They note, for example, that the change to an articular infinitive (τὸ μὴ ὑπερβαίνειν καὶ πλεονεκτεῖν) suggests a new topic; that πλεονεκτεῖν and πρᾶγμα are commercial terms; that Jewish paraenesis frequently links sexual

---

[23]Trans. Danby.

[24]The translations from the *BT* are from the Epstein edition (1935-1948).

[25]Again, one finds similar usage in Greek. Ps-Lucian (*Affairs of the Heart* 19) refers to a woman as "a vessel (δοχεῖον ἀγγεῖον in codices Γ Ε, δοχεῖον alone in the recensions) as it were for the reception of seed." Trans. Macleod. Loeb ed. 1 Peter 3:7 refers to a wife as a "weaker vessel" (ἀσθενέστερον σκεῦος). But this implies that the husband is also a vessel. For this usage in Greek, see Plutarch *Advice* 3 (*Moralia* 138E). Plutarch compares newlyweds to vessels (σκεύη), the sections of which are joined together.

[26]So, for example, Dobschütz 1909, 167, Beauvery 1955, 78-85, and Klassen 1978, 168. Dibelius (1937, 21) and Delling (1968, 271) identify the new topic as lawsuits and disputes in general.

74 Not like the Gentiles

immorality and greediness as the most typical Gentile sins; and that Paul's declaration that "the Lord is an avenging judge *in all these things*" (περὶ πάντων τούτων) implies that more than one issue is addressed.

In response one may argue that the use of the article τό reintroduces the series of infinitives interrupted by "not in the passion of desire as the Gentiles who do not know God"[27] and that "all these things" refers back to the general term "sexual immorality" in v 3b.[28] To be sure, the use of commercial language in v 6 is striking—but no more so than in 1 Cor 7:3-5 where its sexual significance is unmistakable:

Let the husband pay his debt (ὀφειλὴν ἀποδιδότω) to his wife, and let the wife pay her debt to her husband. For the wife does not have controlling rights (ἐξουσιάζειν) over her body. Her husband does. Likewise, the husband does not have controlling rights over his body. His wife does. Do not withhold payment from one another (μὴ ἀποστερεῖτε ἀλλήλους, literally, do not defraud one another) except by mutual agreement (εἰ μήτι ἂν ἐκ συμφώνον) for a specific period of time, so that you may devote yourself to prayer.[29]

Thus, it is not surprising to find commercial language used in the treatment of sexual matters in 1 Thess 4:3-8, even if the precepts Paul cites here are traditional. Indeed, πρᾶγμα and πλεονεκτεῖν are not the only commercial terms in 1 Thess 4:3-8, for σκεῦος κτᾶσθαι itself is language of the market place.

Still, πρᾶγμα is probably not a commercial term in v 6. Nor is it strictly speaking euphemistic. Although πρᾶγμα can mean commercial or legal "business,"[30] it is also a rather common term with no fixed meaning, one which draws its referent from context. In this regard it can refer to various kinds of sexual "affairs." Ronald Hock cites examples in which the

---

[27]Dibelius 1937, 21. Lightfoot (1895, 56) equates τό with ὥστε citing as evidence 1 Thess 3:3 and Phil 4:10. This reading links v 6 directly to v 5.
[28]Best 1972, 165-166. See *Pol Phil.* 5:3, where "abstain from all these things" (ἀπέχεσθαι ἀπὸ πάντων τούτων) follows a list of sexual vices drawn from 1 Cor 6:9-10.
[29]On the use of these terms in contracts, see the relevant entries in Moulton-Milligan 1930. More work needs to be done on Paul's use of commercial language. See Danker 1972, 91-114 for an example of what this might entail and the results which accrue.
[30]Rigaux (1956, 510) and Best (1972, 165-166) point out that the plural is used when πρᾶγμα means "business."

antecedent gives to πρᾶγμα the meaning of pederasty, rape, revel, consorting with prostitutes, and adultery.[31] In other contexts, however, πρᾶγμα can have quite different meanings. Dio Chrysostom, for example, uses it with reference to "theft," of which he had written earlier.[32] The most neutral way of translating ἐν τῷ πράγματι in 1 Thess 4:6, therefore, is simply "in the matter at hand." But following two precepts dealing with sexual morality, it is perhaps better to render it "in the matter of sexual relations."[33]

If, as seems best, one takes πλεονεκτεῖν as an epexegetic infinitive and τὸν ἀδελφὸν αὐτοῦ as the object of both verbs, one may translate 1 Thess 4:6: "Let no man transgress against his brother by defrauding him in the matter of sexual relations."

It is conceivable that "defrauding a brother" is an oblique reference to homosexual acts. Such acts were, of course, common in Greco-Roman society.[34] Indeed, although they were condemned by some, they were for the most part acceptable—at least within certain well-defined social conventions. For the Jews, therefore, homosexual acts characterized the

---

[31] 1982, 44.

[32] Or. 69.8.

[33] The reference to God as an "avenging judge" (ἔκδικος) further suggests that v 6 is concerned with sexual matters. Hock (1982, 52) refers to the romance literature which frequently speaks of the king as an avenging judge in sexual matters. But I still think the parallels from Jewish literature are closer to Paul's usage here. As Hock observes, commentators usually cite Ps 93:1 (LXX) to explain v 6b. (See, for example, Best 1972, 167.) It is in the prophetic literature, however, that God's role as an avenging judge in sexual matters is most prevalent. Linking idolatry and immorality, Hosea cries, "I will punish (ἐκδικήσω) her [Israel] for the feast day of Baals when she burned incense to them . . . and went after her lovers and forgot me, says the Lord" (2:13; See also 4:9-11). Jeremiah echoes this: "How can I pardon you? Your children have forsaken me, and have sworn by those who are no gods. When I fed them to the full, they committed adultery and trooped to the houses of harlots. There were well-fed lusty stallions, each neighing for his neighbor's wife. Shall I not punish them for these things? says the Lord; and shall I not avenge myself (ἐκδικήσει) on a nation like this?" (5:7-9) Later the theme of God's vengeance in sexual matters occurs without reference to idolatry. In Sir 23:16-27 the "fornicator" (πόρνος) and "adulterer" (μοιχός) will be judged (ἐκδικηθήσεται) by God.

[34] In addition to the older literature on homosexuality in the Greco-Roman world, see now Boswell 1980 and Scroggs 1983.

immorality of the Gentile world, so that references to them frequently appear in Jewish apologetic writings.[35] Following Jewish practice, Paul includes homosexual acts in his vice lists[36] and in Rom 1:27 refers to "men committing shameless acts with men" (ἄρσενες ἐν ἄρσεσιν τὴν ἀσχημοσύνην κατεργαζόμενοι) as one result of the Gentiles' failure to acknowledge God.

Πλεονεκτεῖν, however, suggests that the precept is concerned with adultery, for adultery was a crime against the husband. As Ronald Hock points out, in the moral tradition of the Greco-Roman world adultery involves a breach of δικαιοσύνη, the discussions of which frequently include treatment of πλεονεξία.[37] Furthermore, since the second precept in this list deals with "obtaining a wife" as a means of avoiding immorality, it seems likely that the precept concerned with defrauding a brother is also related to marriage.

It is of course impossible to be certain in translating a passage such as 1 Thess 4:3-8, for as we have seen there are serious exegetical problems at every point. But I suggest that, on the basis of the exegesis just offered, there is good evidence for the following translation, which will be the basis of our evaluation of the formulation and function of the precepts in these verses:

(1) Abstain from sexual immorality;

(2) Let each man know how to obtain his own wife;

(3) Let no man transgress against his brother by defrauding him in the matter of sexual relations.

THE FORMULATION AND FUNCTION OF THE PRECEPTS IN 1 THESS 4:3-8

The formulation of the precepts in 1 Thess 4:3-8—short admonitions loosely linked together—is typical of paraenesis in both Jewish and Greco-

---

[35]For examples, see above p 10.

[36]1 Cor 6:9-10. See 1 Tim 1:10. On Boswell's objections to the translation of ἀρσενοκοῖται as "homosexuals" (1980, 341-353), see Scroggs 1983, 106-109.

[37]1982, 45.

Roman literature.[38] Furthermore, the paraenetic traditions of both worlds address marriage and sexual morality in terms very similar to Paul's. They, too, condemn sexual immorality of various kinds, warn against marrying for the sake of pleasure, and renounce adultery. We have already noted the close similarities between 1 Thess 4:3b-5 and Tob 4:12 and *T. Levi* 9:9-10. The proscription against adultery was of course fundamental in Jewish paraenesis, being one of the Ten Commandments.[39]

In the Greco-Roman moral tradition Musonius' diatribe *On Sexual Indulgence* stands out, for here Musonius argues that all sexual relations outside marriage are to be avoided—whether they be with another man's wife, a slave-girl, or another man. Similarly, in his diatribe *What is the Chief End of Marriage?* Musonius insists that one should not marry for wealth, status, or pleasure, but for the common life and the procreation of children.[40] Thus, one can only conclude that there is nothing formally or materially distinctive about the precepts in 1 Thess 4:3-8 themselves.

As we noted above, however, there is another element in Paul's formulation of the precepts he rehearses in 1 Thess 4:3-8—the assertions made about them. These claims attribute the precepts to God, distinguish from the surrounding world those who know God and follow his precepts, and demonstrate the significance of following God's precepts for the internal order of the community of believers. Although we will even find parallels to these claims in other paraenetic traditions, it is by examining this aspect of Paul's formulation of the precepts that we will be able to determine the distinctive character of Paul's paraenesis, which will in turn allow us to discover the significance of the precepts for the Thessalonian community and their function within the letter Paul addressed to it.

(1) Paul reminded the Thessalonians in the introductory thanksgiving period that he and his co-workers had taught each of them one by one (ἕνα ἕκαστον) "to lead a life worthy of God (εἰς τὸ περιπατεῖν . . . ἀξίως τοῦ θεοῦ), who calls you into his own kingdom and glory" (2:11-12). The seriousness with which he viewed the paraenetic aspect of his mission is illustrated by the building up of terms in 2:12: "we exhorted and encour-

---

[38]There are many examples of loosely connected precepts in the *Testaments of the Twelve Patriarchs*. See, for example, *T. Reub.* 3:9-6:5; *T. Sim.* 5:2-3; and *T. Jud.* 18:2-19:1. See also Tob 4:5-21. In the Greco-Roman moral literature, see the paraenetic letters of Isocrates, *To Demonicus* and *To Nicocles*.
[39]Ex 20:14.
[40]On Musonius, see above, pp 47 n 81, and 55.

aged and solemnly charged you" (παρακαλοῦντες ὑμᾶς καὶ παραμυθού-
μενοι καὶ μαρτυρόμενοι). In 4:1-12, Paul underscores the importance of
his moral teaching by continual reference to God as its source. He claims
that the precepts he cites express God's will (v 3a), so that to follow them
is pleasing to God (v 1). The foundation on which they are based is God's
call to holiness (v 7); God's judgment is their measure (v 6b). To disobey
them, therefore, is not to disobey man but God (v 8). Indeed, although
Paul can say that it is he and his co-workers who gave precepts to the
Thessalonians, he claims that they did so "through the Lord Jesus" (διὰ
τοῦ κυρίου 'Ιησοῦ, v 2). The reminder itself comes "in the Lord Jesus"
(ἐν κυρίῳ 'Ιησοῦ, v 1). And finally, Paul tells the Thessalonians that
there is no need for him to instruct them concerning "brotherly love"
because they themselves are "taught by God (θεοδίδακτοι) . . . to love
one another" (v 9). Thus, Paul rehearses seven specific precepts in 1 Thess
4:1-12. But eight times he refers to God (or the Lord Jesus) as their
source. Significantly for our purposes, all but one of these references to
God appear in vv 1-8. The special nature of these precepts for Paul and
his followers, therefore, is clear: They come from God and to follow them
is God's will.

Closely related to Paul's stressing that these precepts represent the
will of God is his emphasizing that the Thessalonians themselves are the
people of God. Paul demonstrates this in a number of ways. For example,
he addresses the letter "to the church of the Thessalonians in God the
Father and the Lord Jesus Christ" (τῇ ἐκκλησίᾳ Θεσσαλονικέων ἐν θεῷ
πατρὶ καὶ κυρίῳ 'Ιησοῦ Χριστῷ, 1:1). He refers to the Thessalonians as
"brethren beloved by God" (ἀδελφοὶ ἠγαπημένοι ὑπὸ τοῦ θεοῦ) and
assures them of their "election" (ἡ ἐκλογή, 1:4). He reminds them that
they have turned from idols to serve the living and true God and that they
await God's son Jesus, who will deliver them from the wrath to come (1:9-
10). And his prayer for the Thessalonians is that they may stand "unblamable in holiness before our God and Father at the coming of our Lord
Jesus with all his saints" (3:13; see also 5:23-24).

A less direct way Paul uses to identify the Thessalonians as the people
of God is to remind them of the boundaries that exist between them and
the world. In the first instance, he does this by referring to non-believers
as "outsiders" (οἱ ἔξω, 4:12), "the rest of mankind" (οἱ λοίποι, 4:13 and
5:16), and, in language reminiscent of the Essenes,[41] as "sons of night
[and] darkness" (νυκτὸς [καὶ] σκότους, 5:5). More important for our

---

[41]See, for example, 1 QM 1:1 and 13:5-6. Compare Col 1:12-14.

purposes, however, in 4:5 he refers to the distinction between believers and non-believers by designating the latter "the Gentiles who do not know God" (τὰ ἔθνη τὰ μὴ εἰδότα τὸν θεόν).

Another term Paul uses to distinguish believers from non-believers is "holiness" (ἁγιασμός), a term which implies separation from the world. Holiness is an important concept for Paul. Believers are "sanctified in Christ Jesus" (ἡγιασμένοι ἐν Χριστῷ Ἰησοῦ) and "called to be saints."[42] Indeed, ἅγιοι ("saints" or "holy ones") is the term Paul uses most frequently in reference to them.[43] This has important ethical consequences. Believers are to present their bodies as a living sacrifice, holy (ἁγίαν) and acceptable to God.[44] And, as we have seen, Paul's prayer for the Thessalonians is that they might stand "unblamable in holiness" (ἀμέμπτους ἐν ἁγιωσύνῃ) in the final judgment (3:13), a prayer he repeats in his closing benediction (5:23-24). It is not surprising, therefore, that Paul uses "holiness" as the determinative category in outlining the conduct which is appropriate for believers in the area of sexual morality.[45] He refers to it no less than three times in 4:3-8. In addition to exhorting believers to marry "in holiness and honor" (ἐν ἁγιασμῷ καὶ τιμῇ), he introduces the three precepts on sexual morality by declaring, "This is the will of God, your holiness" (Τοῦτο γάρ ἐστιν θέλημα τοῦ θεοῦ, ὁ ἁγιασμὸς ὑμῶν) and justifies the precepts by explaining, "For God has not called us to uncleanness but to holiness" (οὐ γὰρ ἐκάλεσεν ὁ θεὸς ἐπὶ ἀκαθαρσίᾳ ἀλλ' ἐν ἁγιασμῷ). It is this last verse which clearly demonstrates that "holiness" distinguishes believers from those who belong to the world: Believers are known by their "holiness"; those who belong to the world by their "uncleanness." V 7 (along with v 3) also shows how "holiness" identifies the Thessalonians as the people of God: It is God who has called them to it, having established it as his will for them.

As a corollary of the Thessalonians' separation from the world, there exists among them a special relationship, that of "brothers" (ἀδελφοί). And again, this derives from their relationship to God, for in baptism

---

[42]1 Cor 1:2. See also Rom 15:16.

[43]Rom 1:7; 8:27; 12:13; 15:25, 26, 31; 16:2, 15; 1 Cor 6:1, 2; 14:33; 16:1, 15; 2 Cor 1:1; 8:4; 9:1, 12; 13:12; Phil 1:1; 4:21, 22; 1 Thess 3:13; 5:27 (in a number of manuscripts); Phlm 5, 7. See also Eph 1:1, 15, 18; 2:19; 3:8, 18; 4:12; 5:3; 6:18; Col 1:2, 4, 12, 26; 2 Thess 1:10.

[44]Rom 13:9-10.

[45]Carrington (1940) and Selwyn (1946, 369-375) argue that 1 Thess 4:1-12 is an example of early Christian catechetical instruction based on the holiness code of Lev 18.

believers receive adoption into the family of God and can henceforth call
God "Abba, Father" (Gal 3:26-4:6; Rom 8:15-18). Thus, as we have already
noted, Paul addresses the Thessalonians as "brethren beloved by God"
(1:4). Even more striking, however, is Paul's claim that "It is not necessary
for me to write to you concerning "brotherly love" (φιλαδελφία), for you
yourselves are taught by God to love one another (4:9). Paul had already
prayed that the Thessalonians abound in love to one another (ὑμᾶς δὲ ὁ
κύριος πλεονάσαι καὶ περισσεύσαι τῇ ἀγάπῃ εἰς ἀλλήλους καὶ εἰς
πάντας, 3:12). But here in 4:9, he claims that the commandment to do so
comes from God. What is even more striking, however, is that now he
characterizes the love the Thessalonians are to show one another as
"brotherly love." In Greco-Roman usage φιλαδελφία normally designated
only the love one had for a blood relation. Φιλανθρωπία or simply φιλία
was used for love of those outside the family. By substituting the familial
term for the terminology belonging to the *topos On Friendship*, therefore,
Paul again focuses on the special character of the community.[46]

It is in the context of this use of fictive-kinship language that we are
to understand the third precept Paul cites in 1 Thess 4:3-8. For while
there can be no doubt that Paul would condemn adultery with someone
outside the community,[47] in 4:6 he is expressly concerned with its effect
on a brother. To transgress against one's brother by defrauding him in the
area of sexual morality is to break not only the commandment against
adultery, but also the commandment to love one another. And it is the
commandment to love one another which forms the foundation on which
all relations in the community are built.[48]

In 1 Thess 4:1-12, therefore, Paul cites seven specific precepts, precepts which were in fact common in Jewish and Greco-Roman moral
literature. Nevertheless, Paul's formulation of these precepts stresses
that they express God's will.

Clearly, therefore, Paul's reference to "the Gentiles who do not know
God" is not incidental to his purpose in chapters 4 and 5. As is the case
throughout this portion of the letter, his reference to non-believers is a
means of making clear to the Thessalonians the conduct appropriate for
believers. While *they* marry "in the passion of desire," *we* marry "in holiness and honor."

Antipater and Juvenal, among others, attest that many in the Greco-

---

[46]See Malherbe 1983a, 252-253 and the literature cited there.
[47]See 1 Cor 6:9.
[48]Rom 13:9-10.

Roman world did in fact marry for passion, financial gain, or some such reason.[49] Indeed, in his treatise *On Marriage* Antipater explicitly attacks those who do.[50] Nevertheless, as we have seen repeatedly, the moralists demonstrate that a much higher standard also obtained among "the Gentiles who do not know God." Their code decreed that a man choose a wife because of her character and way of life rather than for her beauty or wealth and that he treat her honorably, having sexual relations only for the procreation of children, not for the sake of pleasure. Such a code is clearly in keeping with Paul's rejection of "the passion of desire."

One can argue, of course, that in 1 Thess 4:5 Paul criticizes only those Gentiles who actually married for pleasure or financial gain. But this misses the point. Paul's language is clearly polemical. He makes the contrast between *their* conduct and *ours* in the briefest of terms. Unlike Musonius and Antipater, for example, he says almost nothing in his formulation of these precepts about how "the passion of desire" manifests itself. Nor does he explain what it means to marry "in holiness and honor." But this is the nature of polemic. For Paul, as for the Jewish wisdom tradition, the issue is quite simple: idolatry and sexual immorality are one and same.[51] That is, because Gentiles do not know God (or, according to Rom 1:18-32, because Gentiles do not "acknowledge" God), they are ruled by the passion of desire. By contrast, because believers do know God, they are ruled by the will of God, the content of which is holiness. Thus, although the reference to the Gentiles does serve to determine the conduct appropriate for believers, this cannot be its primary function. If it were, we would expect a more detailed treatment of the precepts governing marriage and sexual morality. I suggest, therefore, that it is in the contrast between *us* and *them* itself that we are to discover the primary function of the reference to "the Gentiles who do not know God" and that the primary function is quite simply to encourage the Thessalonians in their efforts to live worthy of God. Indeed, as we shall now see, to encourage the Thessalonians in their new faith is the primary function of all the claims Paul makes concerning the precepts in 1 Thess 4:1-12, which means that this section of the letter is in complete accord with Paul's purpose in writing to the Thessalonians.

(2) A. D. Nock observed, "The real novelty in Christianity was the motivation which it supplied for good conduct and the abhorrence of past

---

[49]See above pp 46-52.

[50]255, 25-34 von Arnim.

[51]See, for example, Wis 14:12.

bad conduct which it demanded."[52] Expanding on this, Nock listed three specific motives: "fear of God, as in Judaism, devotion to Jesus who had suffered in order that sinlessness might be within one's reach, and love for your fellow Christians, who had like you been delivered from death and sin."[53] As our analysis of Paul's formulation of the precepts on marriage and sexual morality has shown, all three of these themes occur in 1 Thess 4:3-8. Paul claims that these precepts express God's will and that to disobey them means incurring God's wrath, that the precepts were given "in the name of the Lord Jesus," and that breaking them is harmful to one's spiritual brothers. For Paul and his followers, that is, one follows these precepts precisely because they are God's will and because they determine relations within the family of God.

The motivating element in Paul's formulation of the precepts in 1 Thess 4:1-12 stands out because, as A. J. Malherbe notes, "in Paul's eyes and probably in his readers' [it] made his instruction different from the popular philosophical traditions he uses."[54] Thus, even if the moralists claimed on occasion that the moral life is pleasing to God,[55] 1 Thess 4:1-12 is distinct because of the emphasis Paul places on the will of God in his formulation of the precepts. To quote Malherbe again,

> [Paul] insists that Christian ethics be grounded in religion. Philosophical traditions are used, but without their preoccupation with the use of reason or the nature of character development. Paul is concerned with the sanctified rather than the rational life.[56]

Malherbe stresses the theological element in Paul's formulation of the

---

[52]1933, 218.

[53]1933, 219.

[54]1983a, 251.

[55]See, for example, Epictetus 2.18, 19-20, where, discussing how one avoids adultery, Epictetus admonishes, "Make it your wish finally to satisfy your own self, make your wish to appear beautiful in the sight of God (θέλησον καλὸς φανῆναι τῷ θεῷ). Set your desire upon becoming pure (καθαρός) in the presence of your own pure self and of God (καὶ μετὰ τοῦ θεοῦ)." Trans. Oldfather. Loeb ed. Seneca (Ep. Mor. 10) advises Lucilius, "'Live among men as if God beheld you (tanquam deus videat); speak with God as if men were listening.'" Trans. Gummere. Loeb ed. On the question of the relation between religion and morality in the Greco-Roman world, see Malherbe 1983a, 251 and the literature cited in n 52.

[56]1983a, 251.

precepts in 1 Thess 4:1-12. But again, I suggest that Paul's concern with the familial quality of relations within the community is equally important, as Nock suggests. Believers are to love one another not simply because God has commanded them to do so but also because they are brothers. Within the community of believers, that is, love is not φιλαν-θρωπία, it is φιλαδελφία. But here we must press Nock's observation further, for in addition to characterizing the community of believers as the family of God Paul draws direct attention to the boundaries that exist between it and the outside world. That is, he distinguishes between *us* and *them*. And again, his reason for doing so is to motivate the Thessalonians.

To distinguish between *us* and *them* serves to motivate a group such as Paul's followers in Thessalonica because, as Nock himself states earlier in the work just cited, conversion was a radical step among early Christians.[57] It did not mean adherence to yet another cult or philosophical school among the many to which one might pledge allegiance. It meant, rather, a complete rejection of all these in favor of the one new faith. Or, to use Paul's own language, it meant turning from idols to serve the living and true God (1 Thess 1:9-10).

Baptism of course was the ritual act which confirmed one as a convert to the new faith. In it, according to 1 Cor 6:11, the believer is washed, sanctified, and justified. In Rom 6, the language is even more striking: Those who have been baptized into Christ Jesus have been baptized into his death, so that having been buried with Christ they might walk in newness of life in keeping with his having been raised from the dead. In Colossians (which was probably not written by Paul, but certainly reflects authentic Pauline traditions) baptism is marked by putting off the old man and putting on the new, symbolized perhaps by stripping away one's clothing before entering the water and donning a new garment upon coming up out of the water.[58] The "newness of life" into which one enters after baptism is characterized by virtue lists (Gal 5:22-23; Col 3:12-13), the old life by vice lists (Gal 5:19-21; 1 Cor 6:9-10; Col 3:8).

The metaphors Paul uses to describe what happens to the believer in baptism, therefore, support Nock's claim that conversion (turning from idols to serve the living and true God) was a radical step. In the language of the sociology of knowledge, a conversion experience of this type involves passing from one social world to another, which means nothing

---

[57] 1933, 164-186.
[58] See Meeks 1983, 150-157.

less than the total realignment of one's perception of reality.[59] Or, to use
Paul's own language again, "If any one is in Christ, the old has passed
away, behold, the new has come" (2 Cor 5:17). Thus, for the man or
woman who was baptized in one of Paul's house churches, the "real" world
was no longer the world defined by Hellenistic culture and ruled by Roman
imperial power. It was the world defined by the house church itself and
ruled by the power of God. Their commonwealth was no longer the city in
which they lived, but the commonwealth in heaven, from which they await
a savior, the Lord Jesus Christ (Phil 3:20).

It is just this total realignment of one's perception of reality which
gives force to Paul's reference to "the Gentiles who do not know God"
when outlining the conduct appropriate for believers in the area of sexual
morality. One follows the precepts Paul lays down not simply because
they are the will of God, but also because they reflect the "real" world as
perceived by the Pauline community. They reflect the way we live in
contrast to the way the rest of the world lives.

While it may cause problems for some to discover that in practical
terms there was no real difference between the Pauline community and
the Hellenistic moralists with regard to sexual morality, it apparently
caused no problems to Paul himself. But again, as Wayne Meeks observes,
Paul was not concerned with an objective description of Greco-Roman
society.[60] His language is polemical. Its purpose was to encourage the
Thessalonians by demonstrating what is involved in being a member of the
community of believers and insisting that to remain within the community
one must conduct oneself in keeping with the standards by which it is
defined. Furthermore, it does not lessen the force of Paul's argument to
say that on occasion the moralists also resort to nativistic slurs, contrasting their own moral conduct with the immorality of barbarians.[61] Indeed,
this simply confirms the polemical nature of such claims. I maintain,
however, that the impact of these claims would be greater for a community such as Pauline Christianity because the boundaries between it and

---

[59] See Berger-Luckmann 1966. Baptism, therefore, was a rite of
passage. But as Meeks (1983, 157) points out, it was not a passage "from
one status to another within a small homogenous society: from child to
man, from elder to chief . . . because the group which the initiate enters
does not entirely share the same symbolic world from which he comes."

[60] 1983, 101.

[61] Maximus of Tyre, for example, contrasts the goodness and beauty
associated with Platonic love to the base and foreign love of pleasure
(*Philosophumena* 19 Hobein). Other examples in Hock 1982, 53.

the world were more sharply defined than those between Greeks and barbarians. After all, Pauline Christianity was a minor element within the macrosociety of the Greco-Roman world, composed for the most part of people who would have been considered barbarians. Thus, Paul's reference to the Gentiles who do not know God was another means of motivating the Thessalonians.

(3) Paul's claims that the precepts he cites reflect God's will, are given in the name of the Lord Jesus, determine relations within the community of believers, and define the boundaries of this community doubtless serve, in the first instance at least, to motivate the Thessalonians to follow the precepts he actually lists in 1 Thess 4:1-12. I suggest, however, that his main purpose was not so narrowly focused. This suggestion stems from an important series of articles by A. J. Malherbe.[62] In these articles Malherbe demonstrates that 1 Thessalonians is a paraenetic letter. That is, such phrases as καθὼς οἴδατε (1:5; 2:2, 5; 3:4), καθάπερ οἴδατε (2:11), and οἴδατε (2:1; 3:3; 4:2; 5:2); reference to models to be imitated (1:6; 2:14; 5:7); the use of the antithetical οὐ . . . ἀλλά (2:1-8); the claim that the letter is a substitute for Paul's own presence (3:6, 10); and Paul's likening himself to a father (2:11-12) and a nurse taking care of her own children (2:7)—all are features of paraenetic literature. This suggests, according to Malherbe, that 1 Thessalonians 1-3 is paraenetic and not apologetic, as most scholars have claimed. Thus, the whole letter (and not simply chapters 4 and 5) is paraenetic. Its purpose was to encourage recent converts to continue doing what they were already doing—remaining faithful to the gospel Paul had proclaimed and living in a way that was pleasing to God.

If 1 Thessalonians is a paraenetic letter, the purpose of which is general exhortation, we are forced back to the question raised at the beginning of this chapter: Why does Paul consider it important to remind the Thessalonians of precepts regarding marriage and sexual morality? I suggest that he did so precisely because for Paul these precepts epitomized the distinction that exists between the world and the community of believers and that consequently they were especially relevant for inclusion in a letter of general exhortation.

So far in our consideration of the function of the precepts in 1 Thess

---

[62]1968, 1970, 1983b, and the forthcoming article "Hellenistic Moralists and the New Testament," which incorporates his paper "1 Thessalonians as a Paraenetic Letter" read at the SBL Seminar on Paul in Los Angeles in 1972.

4:3-8 we have concentrated on Paul's formulation of the precepts on marriage and sexual morality in light of the Hellenistic moralists. This has allowed us to highlight the distinctive features of Paul's formulation. In wrestling with the problem of translating these precepts, however, we noted two passages in the Jewish paraenetic tradition which are formally almost identical to 1 Thess 4:3b-5: Tob 4:12 and *T. Levi* 9:9-10. The similarity between these two precepts and 1 Thess 4:3b-5 is not simply formal, however. Like 1 Thess 4:3b-5, they also serve to distinguish the community (in this case the Jewish community of the diaspora) from the surrounding world. This, as we saw in the chapter surveying Jewish precepts on marriage and sexual morality, was a predominant theme in Jewish paraenesis of the diaspora. Thus, while there *are* striking similarities between Paul's precepts and those of the Greco-Roman moralists, it is the Jewish tradition which determined Paul's formulation of the precepts on marriage and sexual morality.[63] He uses them, that is, to distinguish believers from non-believers.

Using the precepts on marriage and sexual morality in this way accords with Paul's purpose in writing to the Thessalonians because calling attention to the special character of their community was itself a means of exhorting them. The Thessalonians, after all, were recent converts.[64] And one way of encouraging recent converts to continue in their new life is to remind them again and again of who they are and that what they do is a reflection of who they are.

I suggest, finally, that an examination of the other precepts in 1 Thess 4:1-12 confirms this reading of the precepts on marriage and sexual morality. For by reminding the Thessalonians that the love they show to one another is "brotherly love" and that they should aspire to live quietly, mind their own affairs, and work with their own hands so that they may command the respect of "outsiders" and be in need of nothing also calls attention to the special character of the community.[65]

Thus, Paul does not remind the Thessalonians of his precepts on marriage and sexual morality because the Thessalonians had resorted to

---

[63]The Jewish paraenetic tradition of the diaspora was itself dependent on the paraenetic literature of the Greco-Roman world. This needs to be examined further. The most recent attempt to do so is Collins 1983, 137-174.

[64]Elpidius Pax (1971 and 1972) also emphasizes that 1 Thessalonians was addressed to recent converts.

[65]On the nature of these precepts, see Malherbe 1977b, 25-27 and Hock 1980, 42-47.

immoral practices associated with their former worship of idols or were in danger of doing so. He is not answering questions brought to him by Timothy. Nor does he address these issues simply because they were standard topics in the Greco-Roman moral tradition. He refers to marriage and sexual morality because the traditional formulation of the precepts he knew distinguished believers from non-believers and citing them would remind the Thessalonians of who they were, which would in turn encourage them to continue their efforts to lead a life that is pleasing to God. Paul employs traditional polemic concerning marriage, that is, in the service of general paraenesis.

There is, of course, a potential problem in emphasizing the distinctive character of the community of believers. It may lead to the conclusion that believers should completely separate themselves from the outside world. There is no indication that the Thessalonians drew this conclusion (assuming 2 Thessalonians to be authentically Pauline). Some in Corinth, however, did. Indeed, it may well be that the Corinthians came to this conclusion based on the kind of argument Paul used in his letter to the Thessalonians. But this brings us to the consideration of Paul's treatment of marriage and sexual morality in 1 Corinthians, to which we now turn.

4
Adapting the Precepts
to a New Situation

Paul's treatment of marriage in 1 Corinthians 7 begins with a maxim: "It is good for a man not to touch a woman" (καλὸν ἀνθρώπῳ γυναῖκος μὴ ἅπτεσθαι, v 1b). He immediately qualifies it, however, by adding, "But because of sexual immorality, let each man have his own wife, and let each woman have her own husband" (διὰ δὲ τὰς πορνείας ἕκαστος τὴν ἑαυτοῦ γυναῖκα ἐχέτω, καὶ ἑκάστη τὸν ἴδιον ἄνδρα ἐχέτω, v 2). As we have seen, this reservation recalls the first two precepts Paul rehearsed in the paraenetic reminder of 1 Thess 4:1-12. But here in 1 Corinthians 7 Paul makes a number of changes in the way he formulates these precepts: He uses less metaphorical language (γυνή rather than σκεῦος); he speaks of "having" (ἔχειν) a wife (or husband) rather than of "obtaining" (κτᾶσθαι) one; he states explicitly that marriage guards against the dangers of sexual immorality ("Because of sexual immorality (διὰ δὲ τὰς πορνείας), let each man have his own wife ..."); he addresses both men and women ("Let each man ... let each woman ..."); and he omits the phrase "in holiness and honor not in the passion of desire, as the Gentiles who do not know God." All of these changes are significant. They reflect the new situation Paul is addressing. Thus, examining them gives us insight into the way Paul adapts traditional precepts as new situations demand different responses.

We concluded in the last chapter that in 1 Thessalonians 4 Paul did not cite the precepts on marriage and sexual morality because there was a specific problem in Thessalonica, but because the traditional formulation of these precepts distinguished the community of believers from the surrounding world and because reminding the Thessalonians of this distinction served well his purpose in writing to them—to reinforce their efforts to persevere and grow in their new faith. In 1 Corinthians, however, Paul *was* dealing with a specific problem, or more precisely, with several specific problems. In the first instance, he had received a letter from the Corinthians inquiring, in part, about matters related to marriage and sexual morality.[1] Chapter 7 is his response to this inquiry. But Paul had also received an oral report[2] indicating that there was flagrant sexual immorality within the community: a man was engaging in sexual relations with his step-mother, a form of immorality taboo even among the Gentiles (5:1).[3] Paul dealt with the case of incest in no uncertain terms. He charged the assembled community to cast the man out (5:4) and ridiculed those who were "puffed up" in their claim to superior wisdom for being unable to deal with the problem (5:2 and 6).[4] It is striking that although Paul is concerned with the salvation of the man's spirit (v 5b), his greater concern is with the purity of the community.[5] This becomes clear in vv 6-8. Since

---

[1]Paul first mentions the Corinthians' letter in 7:1: "Now concerning the things about which you wrote" (περὶ δὲ ὧν ἐγράψατε). Most scholars find further references to this letter in 7:25; 8:1; 12:1; 16:1 and 12, where in each instance Paul introduces a new topic with the phrase "now concerning" (περι δε). In addition to marriage and sexual morality, therefore, the Corinthians inquired concerning food offered to idols, spiritual gifts, the contributions for the saints, and Apollos.

[2]In 1:11 Paul indicates that the report concerning the quarrels in Corinth comes from Chloe's people (ὑπὸ τῶν Χλόης). In 16:17 he refers to a visit from Stephanas, Fortunatus, and Achaicus, whom many scholars consider an official delegation charged with the delivery of the letter to Paul (see, for example, Hurd 1965, 50 and Dahl 1977, 50). Here in 5:1 (and in 11:18 where he refers to the divisions which obtain at the celebration of the Lord's Supper), however, Paul does not name his source. Thus, it is impossible to determine who provided Paul with this information. It may well be that both Chloe's people and the Corinthian delegation spoke to Paul of this issue.

[3]It is unclear whether the man was married to his step-mother or kept her as a concubine. The present tense of ἔχειν indicates at any rate that it was a continuing relationship. Since, according to the Institutes of Gaius 1.63, marriage between a man and his step-mother was forbidden by law and since concubinatus was frequently the resort of people who could not marry for legal reasons, it may well be that the couple was not married. If this was the case, ἔχειν is to be taken as a euphemism for sexual intercourse. On ἔχειν in 1 Cor 7:2, see below p 97.

[4]The Corinthians are not "puffed up" because of this situation, but in spite of it. See below pp 117-122.

[5]Note that Paul never addresses the man himself. All of his advice is to the community.

"a little leaven leavens the whole lump," Paul urges the community to "cleanse out the old leaven that you may be a new lump, as you really are unleavened." His attempt to clarify an earlier letter which had been misinterpreted by the Corinthians carries this argument further. In this letter Paul had written that believers should not associate with "the immoral" (πόρνοι). The Corinthians had evidently taken this to mean that they should avoid immoral persons outside the community. Paul now explains, however, that by "the immoral" he had meant those who claimed to be a "brother" and yet persisted in immorality, avarice, idolatry, etc., concluding that such persons should be driven out of the community (v 13).[6] In 6:9-11 Paul again refers to the purity of believers. Alluding to a baptismal formula he reminds the Corinthians that the immoral, idolaters, adulterers, etc., will not inherit the kingdom of God. Then he recalls that while some of them had in fact been such, they are now washed, sanctified, and justified in the name of the Lord Jesus.[7] And again, when addressing the Corinthians' abuse of the slogan "All things are lawful for me," his concern is with the purity of the community. To be sure Paul does not use purity language in 6:12-20, but the imagery of the body suggests that this is what he has in mind.[8] For he argues that to join oneself to a prostitute is to become one body with her, which the believer must not do since he has joined himself to the Lord and become one spirit with him.[9]

This whole argument about the purity of the community of believers, of course, is in keeping with Paul's advising the Thessalonians to live in

---

[6]Paul cites Deut 17:7. Note, however, that he substitutes the plural for the singular of the Greek text of the OT. Again, his advice is to the whole community.

[7]Vv 9-11 conforms to the "soteriological contrast pattern," which "is intended to help believers understand what the existence newly offered to them in Christ really means and entails, in contrast to their former life as pagans or Jews" (Dahl 1976, 33-34).

[8]See the work of anthropologist Mary Douglas (especially 1973 and 1974, 93-112) for a discussion of the use of body language as an expression of group boundaries and social control. Douglas's essays are having a growing impact on the analysis of early Christianity. See, for example, Meeks 1979.

[9]It is possible that some of the Corinthians visited prostitutes, claiming that "all things are lawful." (See, for example, Barrett [1982, 13] and Bruce [1977, 261].) More likely, however, Paul describes in 6:12-20 the extremes to which the slogan "all things are lawful" can bring one when improperly applied. See Hurd 1965, 277 and Meeks, 1983, 129.

holiness and honor not in the passion of desire, as the Gentiles who do not know God. Indeed, in 6:18 he even cites one of the rules he had given to the Thessalonians: "Flee sexual immorality" (φεύγετε τὴν πορνείαν). There is a difference, however, between Paul's use of purity language in 1 Thessalonians and 1 Corinthians, for in the former letter its purpose is exhortation; in the latter its purpose is chastisement. That is, although the language of purity in 1 Corinthians does reflect the boundaries which exist between believers and non-believers (as it did in 1 Thessalonians), Paul is more concerned with the internal order of the Corinthian community. The impurity which threatens the community is not from outside but from within.

In 1 Corinthians, moreover, Paul must deal with the misunderstanding of an earlier letter to this congregation. Thus, he argues that believers cannot separate themselves completely from immoral persons outside the community, since to do so would mean withdrawing from society.[10] In spite of his desire that the Corinthians set up their own courts to deal with disputes which arise within the community (6:1-8), Paul never advocates so radical a step as withdrawal from society. His goal, rather, is to maintain the purity of the community *and* to draw others into it.[11]

Having dealt with the oral report, Paul turns his attention to the Corinthians' letter. It is tempting to reconstruct this letter and then to analyze Paul's discussion in light of it. But since reconstructing the Corinthians' letter depends for the most part on how one reads Paul's reply, this puts the methodological cart before the horse. Thus, we must exercise caution in this task. As it is, we have only two relatively clear references to the letter in chapter 7: The maxim "it is good for a man not to touch a woman" (v 1b) and the formula "now concerning" (περὶ δέ) in v 25 which introduces a new topic, namely, "the virgins" (αἱ παρθένοι).

Because of the difficulties in reconstructing the Corinthians' letter, I will begin here with an analysis of Paul's argument and only then attempt to determine what the Corinthians asked in their letter and why these particular issues arose. Moreover, although v 25 does appear to reflect a new topic, I will treat Paul's argument in chapter 7 as a whole, since the

---

[10]On this, see Meeks 1979.

[11]This becomes clear in Paul's discussion of mixed marriages (7:12-16), for here Paul advises those who are married to non-believers not to seek divorce since there is a possibility that they may win their non-believing spouse. For support of this reading of v 16, see below pp 112-113.

tradition he cites in v 2 has a bearing on his response to the question concerning the virgins as well as on the issues raised in vv 1-24.

Although I will postpone discussion of the Corinthians' letter to Paul, there is one aspect of this discussion so crucial to determining Paul's response that it must be treated now, namely, whether 7:1b is a Corinthian slogan or a Pauline dictum.

"IT IS GOOD FOR A MAN NOT TO TOUCH A WOMAN"— A CORINTHIAN SLOGAN OR PAULINE RESPONSE?

As we have noted, the traditional rules Paul cites in v 2 offer a contrast to the maxim in v 1b. Nevertheless, many scholars argue that "it is good for a man not to touch a woman" does in fact represent Paul's own view and that it is his response to one of the Corinthians' questions.[12] These scholars point out, for example, that vv 7, 8, 27, 32-35, and 40 express a point of view similar to that of v 1b; that the use of καλόν reflects Pauline style; and that there is no introductory formula to indicate that the maxim is a Corinthian slogan.

A growing number of scholars, however, regard "it is good for a man not to touch a woman" as one of the Corinthians' slogans.[13] The most telling argument in favor of this view is that Paul responds to the maxim in the same manner he responds to the sayings in 8:1, 6:12, and 10:23—all of which are commonly regarded as Corinthian slogans. That is, he quotes the saying as if he agrees with it and then adds strong qualifications to its use.[14] In qualifying the Corinthians' views, moreover, Paul frequently

---

[12]Hurd (1965, 68) provides a chart which catalogues scholarly opinion regarding possible quotations in 1 Corinthians. Of the twenty-four works listed, fourteen regard 7:1b as Pauline. Conzelmann (1975, 114-116), Baltensweiler (1967, 156), and Schüssler Fiorenza (1983, 223) should now be added to the list of scholars who take "it is good for a man not to touch a woman" as a Pauline dictum.

[13]In addition to the ten scholars listed by Hurd (see the previous note), Hurd himself (1965, 163), Barrett (1971, 154), Meeks (1983, 102), Scroggs (1972, 276), Murphy-O'Connor (1981, 603), and Bruce (1977, 267) are among recent commentators who regard 7:1b as a Corinthian slogan. Bruce (1972, 267 n 17) points out that this interpretation of v 1b goes back as far as Origen (*Commentary on I Corinthians* 121).

[14]This point was first made by Jeremias (1953, 151). Interestingly, Musonius' diatribe *Must One Obey One's Parents Under All Circumstances?* is structured in a similar way. Musonius is asked by a young man whose father prohibited his study of philosophy, "Tell me, Musonius, must

employs their own language, thus accounting for his use of καλόν in vv 8 and 26.[15] Furthermore, an examination of Paul's quotations of the Corinthians' slogans reveals that while he does use an introductory formula in 8:1 ("we know that . . ." [οἴδαμεν ὅτι . . .]), on other occasions (at 6:12 and 10:23, for example), he quotes a slogan without any indication that he is doing so. But after all, there is little reason for Paul to demonstrate that he is citing the Corinthians—they were well aware of their own slogans.

To be sure, vv 7, 8, 27, 32-35, and 40 do reflect a point of view similar to that expressed in the maxim in v 1b. But there is a notable difference, for in these verses (with the exception of v 7) the emphasis is on *remaining as you are*, not on abstinence from sexual intercourse. Thus, for example, when treating the question of marriage in vv 8, 27, and 32-35, Paul argues not only that those who are unmarried (whether single, widowed, or divorced) should remain unmarried, but also that those who are married should remain married.[16]

On balance, therefore, it seems more likely that "it is good for a man not to touch a woman" was a slogan expressing the view of some of the believers of Corinth. We are still, however, left with the question of what it meant.

In both Hebrew and Greek "to touch a woman" is a euphemism for sexual intercourse.[17] Thus, on first reading 7:1b appears to be a rejection

---

one obey one's parents in all things, or are there some circumstances under which one need not heed them?" (100, 20-22 Lutz. Trans. Lutz.) Musonius' initial response indicates that it is indeed "good" (καλόν) to obey one's father and mother and that he recommends it. Then, however, Musonius discusses the question further, describing situations in which it would be proper *not* to obey one's parents.

[15]See, for example, his discussion of "wisdom" (σοφία) in chapters 1-4. On the nuances in Paul's use of σοφία, see Barrett 1982, 6-14.

[16]Moreover, the excursus on circumcision and slavery in vv 17-24 demonstrates that Paul's primary emphasis in chapter 7 is on remaining as you are, not on abstinence from sexual intercourse. That is, the excursus (like the one in chapter 9) serves to bolster the argument Paul is putting forward. See Bartchy 1973, chapter 4.

[17]See Gen 20:6 and Prov 6:29 where the LXX translates the Hebrew גלל with forms of ἅπτω. Liddell and Scott (See under ἅπτω 5) cite Plato's *Laws* 840a and Aristotle's *Politics* 1335b 40 as examples of the Greek usage. The latter is especially important, since it states that "As to intercourse with another woman or man, in general *it must be dishonourable* to be known to take any part in it in any circumstances whatsoever

of all sexual intercourse. Because Paul's initial response to the slogan deals with marriage and sexual intercourse within marriage, however, some scholars argue that the slogan itself deals with these issues and not with sexual intercourse alone.[18] But Paul's responding to the slogan in these terms does not mean that it cannot be taken at face value, even if the Corinthians also claimed that believers should not marry and that those who were married should not engage in sexual relations. Indeed, as we shall see, it is probable that these claims grow out of the more general rejection of all sexual intercourse. Thus, it seems best to take the slogan at face value, that is, as a rejection of all sexual relations.

Another problem in understanding the slogan is the characterization of abstinence from all sexual intercourse as "good" (καλόν). Tertullian, who took v 1b as Paul's view, claimed that since it is good for a man not to touch a woman, it is by implication wrong to touch a woman.[19] Most modern commentators, however, are less radical, arguing that καλόν is to be taken pragmatically (that is, as expressing no moral judgment)[20] or as "the goal of morality, the highest member of a series of lesser 'goods.'"[21] All too frequently, however, scholars weaken the sense of καλόν simply to avoid the embarrassment of having to argue that Paul had a very low opinion of marriage and sexual intercourse.[22] But if v 1b does in fact represent the view of some of the Corinthians who had taken a very rigoristic stance with regard to sexual intercourse, there is no reason to take καλόν in anything less than absolute terms. And if some in Corinth were advocating that married persons should abstain from sexual inter-

---

as long as one is a husband and bears that name" (περὶ δὲ τῆς πρὸς ἄλλην ἢ πρὸς ἄλλον, ἔστω μὲν ἁπλῶς μὴ καλὸν ἁπτόμενον φαίνεσθαι μηδαμῇ μηδαμῶς ὅταν ᾖ καὶ προσαγορευθῇ πόσις). Trans. Rackham, Loeb ed.

[18]See, for example, Allo 1935; 153-154; Grosheide 1953, 155; and Meyer 1881, 193.

[19]On Monogamy 4.60. See also, Jerome Against Jovian 1.7.

[20]See, for example, Bachmann 1921, 254; Héring 1962, 49; Morris 1958, 105; and Grosheide 1953, 154-155.

[21]See, for example, Lietzmann-Kümmel 1949, 29; Allo 1935, 153-154; Moffatt 1938, 73-76; and Wendland 1962, 49. The quotation is Hurd's characterization of this position (1965, 159).

[22]Typical of this view is Craig (1951, vol 10, 76-77): "It is regrettable that Paul, the bachelor, should have ignored so completely all other aspects of the companionship of married couples and should have written as if marriage were little more than legalized cohabitation."

course (as indeed seems the case),[23] it is probable that their intention was to express the absolute moral good. Thus, "it is good for a man not to touch a woman" refers only to sexual intercourse and is probably a complete rejection of it. This brings us then to Paul's response.

PAUL'S RESPONSE:
THE REFORMULATION OF TRADITION

Since Paul had already dealt with the question of sexual intercourse outside of marriage (6:12-20), he focuses attention here on the place of sexual intercourse within marriage. In 1 Thess 4:3b-4 Paul had simply juxtaposed the two precepts on marriage and sexual morality: "Abstain from sexual immorality. Let each man obtain his own wife . . ." As we saw, this implies that marriage is a means of guarding oneself against immorality. In 1 Cor 7:2, however, Paul makes this explicit by subordinating the first precept, making it the reason for the second: "*Because of* sexual immorality (διὰ δὲ τὰς πορνείας), let each man have his own wife and let each woman have her own husband." As many commentators point out, Paul may have had in mind the sexual immorality that actually obtained in Corinth when he advised believers to marry "because of sexual immorality."[24] There is little evidence in 1 Corinthians, however, that sexual immorality was in fact a major problem in the Corinthian community. The only clear instance is the case of incest mentioned in 5:1. Moreover, the boasting Paul ridicules here should not be taken as evidence of a

---

[23]See below pp 117-122.

[24]See, for example, Barrett 1971, 155-156. Many scholars (most recently Bruce 1977, 249) point out that Corinth had the reputation of being an immoral city. As evidence they cite Plato's reference to "Corinthian courtesans" (*Republic* 404D), Aristophanes' use of "to play the Corinthian" for "to fornicate" (frgm 354), "The Whoremonger" (ὁ Κορινθιαστής) as the title of plays by Philetaerus and Poliochus (listed by Athenaeus in *The Deipnosophists* 13.559a and 7.313c respectively), Strabo's maxim "It is not for every man to make a voyage to Corinth," and his description of the temple of Aphrodite in Corinth as so rich that it had in its service more than a thousand cultic prostitutes (*Geog.* 8.378; Loeb ed.: 4.191). Conzelmann (1967, 247-261), however, argues that all of these refer to the ancient city of Corinth and reflect Athenian anti-Corinth propaganda. There is no evidence that the Corinth of Paul's day (The city was destroyed by the Romans in 146 B.C.E. and refounded by Julius Caesar in 44 B.C.E.) was more immoral than any other Greco-Roman city.

libertine party which takes pride in the man's freedom. The point of chapter 5 is, rather, that the Corinthians' claim to superior knowledge is an empty one because their inability to deal with the case of immorality demonstrates that they are in fact lacking in wisdom. To be sure, Paul condemns consorting with prostitutes in 6:12-20. But it is by no means clear that the Corinthians were actually visiting prostitutes. It seems more likely that Paul's purpose in 6:12-20 is to describe the depths to which the principle "all things are lawful" will carry one when improperly applied. That is, the discussion of consorting with prostitutes is a *reductio ad absurdum*.[25] Thus, in linking the warning against sexual immorality with advice on having a wife or husband, Paul is simply following the tradition which he had already cited in 1 Thessalonians 4:4.

If it is correct to take 1 Cor 7:2 as another rehearsal of the traditional precepts cited in 1 Thessalonians 4, we should read ἔκαστος τὴν ἑαυτοῦ γυναῖκα ἐχέτω ("let each man have his own wife") as "let each man be married." Some scholars reject this reading, however, claiming that ἔχειν here is a euphemism for sexual intercourse.[26] This use of ἔχειν was in fact current in Paul's world and, as the scholars who take this view point out, Paul appears to use it this way in 5:1.[27] Nevertheless, in 7:12-13 and 29 Paul refers to "having" a wife (or husband) with no explicit sexual connotation. Moreover, if ἔχειν γυναῖκα (ἄνδρα) does refer to sexual intercourse in 7:2, Paul must be seen as making the same point three different times in vv 2, 3-4, and 5, which is possible but unlikely. Again, therefore, it appears that in v 2 Paul is following the tradition and speaks simply of "having a wife (or husband)." Here in 1 Corinthians, he substitutes "having" for "obtaining" because in vv 2-7 his concern is not so much with *whether* one should marry (He will take up this question in vv 8-10 and vv 25-40.) but with the place of sexual intercourse within marriage. Thus, v 2 qualifies the Corinthians' slogan and provides a transition to his treatment of marriage, the one context in which Paul sees sexual intercourse as not only appropriate but obligatory.

Vv 3-5, therefore, is Paul's more explicit rebuttal of the Corinthians' slogan. Sexual intercourse, he argues, is in fact an obligation (ὀφειλή) married persons owe one another. They may abstain from it only for a short time (πρὸς καιρόν) and for a specific reason—to dedicate them-

---

[25]See below pp 117-122.
[26]See, for example, von Campenhausen 1957, 21 n 2; Hurd 1965, 162.
[27]See above n 3.

selves to prayer (ἵνα σχολάσητε τῇ προσευχῇ). He insists further that even this withdrawal from one another be by mutual consent (ἐκ συμφώνου), and that after the agreed upon period has passed, the couple must resume sexual relations, lest Satan tempt them because of their incontinence (ἵνα μὴ πειράζῃ ὑμᾶς ὁ σατανᾶς διὰ τὴν ἀκρασίαν ὑμῶν). Taken by itself, Paul's argument in vv 3-5 is a clear rejection of the Corinthians' position—at least with regard to sexual relations between married persons. Vv 6-7, however, raise serious problems for understanding just how Paul regarded this advice, for he continues:

> But I say this by way of concession, not of command. But I desire that all be as I am myself. Yet each person has his own gift from God—one of one kind and another of another.

How are vv 6-7 related to the argument of vv 3-5? Answering this question depends, in part at least, on how one answers another, namely, What is the concession Paul makes here? But answering this question depends on how one answers yet another: To what does "this" (τοῦτο) in v 6 refer?

In vv 26 and 29 τοῦτο refers to what follows. One can read it this way in v 6 also, if, as may well be the case, the Corinthians had based their position in part at least on Paul's own life and had indicated this in their letter. Thus, one would read vv 6-7:

> I concede that I desire all to be as I am myself, as you suggest. But I cannot make this a command, for each person has his own gift from God. Some in accordance with mine, but others of a different kind.

Without specific knowledge of the Corinthians' letter, however, it is impossible to provide adequate justification for such a reading. Thus, scholars generally take τοῦτο as referring to what precedes and see the concession as (a) marriage itself, (b) sexual intercourse within marriage, (c) abstaining from sexual intercourse to devote oneself to prayer, or (d) resuming sexual intercourse after a time of abstinence for prayer.

Of these possibilities (d) is least likely, since it undermines the case Paul has just made in vv 3-4. Similarly, if Paul considers (b) a concession, he appears to be sanctioning a kind of "spiritual marriage." This, of course, is possible. But it is difficult to see how his referring to sexual relations as a "debt" married persons owe to one another and his claiming that withholding oneself from one's partner is "robbing" him or her would accord with support of spiritual marriages.

Regarding (a) one may argue that, since v 2 does in fact sound like a command, Paul wanted to modify it lest it be interpreted as an absolute rule. This reading of the concession accords with the usual rendering of v 7a: "I should like all to be as I am myself. But each has his own gift from God . . ." C. K. Barrett, however, has argued that "I should like . . ." is a mistranslation, since Paul does not use the imperfect tense, which would express an unattainable wish, but the present tense, which expresses "a wish that is capable of realization, and ought to be realized, . . . almost a command." Thus Barrett translates v 7a, "I desire all men to be as I am myself" and claims that since Paul did expect his wish to be fulfilled he was not referring here to celibacy but (quoting Philipp Bachmann) to "'the capacity for resistance to sensual allurements.'" That is, Paul did not require that everyone be celibate, but he did require that everyone avoid sexual immorality.[28]

If this interpretation of v 7a is correct, it is of course less likely that marriage is the concession to which Paul refers. There is a problem with Barrett's reading of v 7a, however, for although he is correct in pointing out that Paul's use of the present tense suggests that θέλω δὲ πάντας ἀνθρώπους εἶναι ὡς καὶ ἐμαυτόν expresses an attainable wish, reading it this way robs ἀλλά in v 7b of any force. That is, the structure of v 7 demands that we take "but each has his own gift from God . . ." as a contrast to v 7a, which suggests that Paul does in fact desire that all be celibate as he himself is. Thus, if one reads v 6 in close association with v 7, marriage does appear to be the concession Paul makes when he writes "I say this by way of concession not of command."

To link v 6 directly with v 7, however, means disregarding the adversative particle δέ in v 7a. This δέ has been problematic in the interpretation of v 7 from earliest times, as the variant reading demonstrates.[29] But before we pass over it as meaningless, we must look for a reading which accounts for it.

This brings us then to (c), abstaining from sexual intercourse to devote oneself to prayer. V 5b is clearly a concession (εἰ μήτι ἄν). But as J. C. Hurd observes, it is difficult to see how v 5b could ever be taken as a

---

[28] 1971, 158.
[29] ℵ² B D² Ψ and the majority text, along with vg^{cl} sy and Cyprian, have οὖν rather than δέ. Most English translations disregard the δέ in v 7.

command and thus necessitate the qualification Paul makes in v 6.[30] In response, however, it should be noted that there is an implied command in v 5b: In order to devote oneself to prayer, one *must* abstain from sexual intercourse. Taken this way, Paul would be saying in v 6, "you *may* abstain from sexual intercourse when devoting yourself to prayer, but it is not necessary for you to do so." Paul, therefore, would be challenging the notion that sexual intercourse, even in marriage, renders one ritually unclean. This was a basic presupposition in both Jewish and Greco-Roman cultic life, one which doubtless underlies the slogan in v 1b.[31] For Paul to challenge this notion would, of course, be unusual. But it is not without analogy in the moral literature of his time, for in his *Life of Pythagoras* Iamblichus attributes to Theano a similar argument:

> It is holy for a woman, after having been connected with her husband, to perform sacred rites on the same day; but ... it is never holy, after she has been connected with any other man.[32]

If this reading of v 6 is correct, therefore, Paul calls into question not only the Corinthians' slogan but also the presupposition on which it is based.

One of the merits of taking abstinence from sexual intercourse to devote oneself to prayer as the concession Paul makes in v 6 is that it allows one to account for the particle δέ in v 7, since the δέ makes sense only if v 7 refers to something other than v 6. Thus, "I say this by way of concession" qualifies v 5b; and v 7a is not a restatement of v 6, but, as Paul's admission that he does wish that all were celibate as he himself is, a qualification of the whole argument of vv 2-6.

Even so, Paul's admission that he desires all to be celibate does not bring him into agreement with the Corinthians, for as we shall see Paul's concern is not with the content of the Corinthians' slogan, but with their

---

[30]1965, 161-162.

[31]See Ex 19:15; Lev 15:18; and 1 Sam 21:4-6. For the Greco-Roman view, see Plutarch *Table-Talk* 3.6.4 (*Moralia* 655D): "I suppose we must, in obedience to our city's law, guard carefully against rushing into a god's sanctuary and beginning the sacrifices when we have been engaged in any sexual activity a short time before." Trans. Clement. Loeb ed.

[32]Text in Thesleff 1965, 55; trans. Taylor 1818, 96. According to Iamblichus, this Theano was the wife of Brontinus. He notes, however, that some attribute the saying to Theano the wife of Pythagoras.

claim that it applies to everyone, a claim he rejects even as he agrees with the slogan itself.

Still, Paul's primary concern in vv 2-7 is not with the question of whether one should marry but with the Corinthians' claim that all sexual relations are forbidden to believers. It is only in v 8 that he turns his attention to the question of believers' marrying.

IS IT GOOD FOR BELIEVERS TO MARRY?

Four times in vv 8-40 Paul addresses the question of believers' marrying and in each instance he argues against it.[33] In v 8, he says with regard "to the unmarried and the widows" (τοῖς ἀγάμοις καὶ ταῖς χήραις) that "it is good for them to remain [single] as I do" (καλὸν αὐτοῖς ἐὰν μείνωσιν ὡς κἀγώ).[34] Simiarly, in v 38 he argues that although the one who marries does well (καλῶς) the one who does not marry does better (κρεῖσσον).[35] In neither instance, however, does Paul justify his position.

---

[33]As we shall see, however, his No is always qualified.

[34]It is impossible to determine whether Paul had never married or was widowed or divorced. V 8, at any rate, suggests strongly that he was not married at the time of the writing of 1 Corinthians. As Barrett notes (1971, 161), 9:5 is consistent with his not being married, but does not prove it. It simply indicates that he and Barnabas were not accompanied by wives. Jeremias (1926 and 1929) has argued on the basis of rabbinic literature that it would be very unusual for someone so devoted to the law as Paul to have never married. But this is not conclusive. See Fascher (1929) for a response to Jeremias' first article. Hurd (1965, 275) argues that Paul's ascetic position does not accord with his ever having been married, an argument used by many commentators (See, for example, the comment of Craig cited in n 22 above.). But psychological interpretations such as this are not convincing. One could argue just as well that Paul had experienced a difficult marriage and as a result his attitude became soured. Bruce (1977, 270) suggests that it is "possible" that Paul's wife left him when he became a Christian, "that when he 'suffered the loss of all things' for the sake of Christ [Phil 3:8] he lost his wife, too."

[35]Vv 36-38 present a number of notoriously vexing problems: Who is being addressed here? Who are the "virgins"? Of what does the "unseemly behavior" consist? How are we to understand ὑπέρακμος? Does γαμίζειν in v 38 mean "give in marriage" as it normally does, or can it be taken to mean simply "marry"? The resolution of these problems rests on how one takes the passage as a whole. At least four different solutions have been suggested. Paul is addressing (1) fathers who are perplexed about what to do with their daughters who are beyond the normal age for marrying;

In v 40 he returns to the case of widows, arguing now that the widow will be happier (μαχαριωτέρα) if she remains unmarried. Here again, however, he does not indicate how or why she will be happier if she remains unmarried. He does claim, however, that in making this judgment he has the Spirit of God.

It is only in vv 25-35 that Paul attempts to justify his claim that believers should not marry. Taking up the Corinthians' question "concerning the virgins," he states that although he does not have a specific command from the Lord he gives his opinion (γνώμη) as one who by the Lord's mercy has been found trustworthy.[36] His opinion is that "because of the impending distress" (διὰ τὴν ἐνεστῶσαν ἀνάγκην), it is good for each person to remain as he is (καλὸν ἀνθρώπῳ τὸ οὕτως εἶναι)—which means, of course, that those who are not married should remain single.[37]

---

(2) couples who have entered a kind of "spiritual marriage," that is, one in which they refrain from any sexual relations; (3) an engaged couple; and (4) persons who are questioning the place of levirate marriage within the church. Although none of these solutions resolves all the difficulties in interpreting this passage, the third, which has been most persuasively argued by W.G. Kümmel (1954) and Henry Chadwick (1954), is the most likely. (Kümmel discusses other solutions and provides an extensive bibliography.) Whatever the specific situation, however, Paul's advice is clear enough: "The man who is not under compulsion, who has his desires under control, and who decides to keep his virgin as she is does well. So that the one who marries does well and the one who does not marry does better."

[36]The relation between vv 25-35 and vv 36-38 is a matter of scholarly debate. Weiss (1910, 194-195), Enslin (1957, 176-179), Hurd (1965, 176-182), and Chadwick (1954, 266 n 3), for example, regard vv 25-38 as a unit dealing with a special group within the Corinthian community who, though living together, have taken a vow of chastity. Most scholars, however, consider "the virgins" in v 25 as a general term for the unmarried. It is only in v 36, they claim, that Paul takes up the specific situation in Corinth. (See, for example, Grosheide [1953, 182]; Lightfoot [1895, 231]; and Barrett [1971, 173 and 182-185]. There is wide diversity even among these scholars, however, over the issue treated in vv 36-38.) For our purposes, it is not necessay to resolve this debate, since in either case the question is whether the virgins should marry and in both instances Paul's advice is fundamentally the same: It is better to remain as you are; but if you are not married you are free to marry.

[37]Bachmann (1921, 281), Allo (1934, 177) and Wolbert (1981, 119 n 84) take τὸ οὕτως εἶναι as "remain single." Thus, they argue, Paul addresses his argument concerning the impending distress to the unmarried only. As we shall see, however, v 27, which expands upon v 26, militates against this interpretation.

In v 37 Paul uses ἀνάγκη to refer to one's inability to control one's sexual desires and thus argues that it is a reason *for* marrying. Here in v 26, however, ἀνάγκη has a very different meaning. It refers to the "distress" associated with the end of the age, which, Paul claims, is ἐνεστῶσα- —either "present" or "impending."[38] This eschatological theme continues in vv 18b-31, where Paul warns that those who marry will have "tribulations in the flesh" (θλῖψις ἐν σαρκί). Although Paul himself does not spell out what these are, we are probably to see here a reference to the traditional apocalyptic warnings against marriage and the birth of children found, for example, in 4 Ezra 5:8 and 6:12; Enoch 99:5; and Mark 13:17. Paul injects a further sense of urgency in his warning against marrying by adding that "the time has been shortened" (ὁ καιρὸς συνεσταλμένος ἐστίν) and "the form of this world is passing away" (παράγει . . . τὸ σχῆμα τοῦ κόσμου τούτου). Although the immediate conclusion Paul draws from the passing of this age is that those who are married should live as though they were not married,[39] it clearly accords with his argument of vv 25-28 and gives immediacy to his claim that believers should not marry.

In vv 32-35 Paul adduces another argument in favor of remaining unmarried. He turns from eschatological woes to the day-to-day cares of married life:

> I wish you to be free from anxieties (ἀμερίμνους). The unmarried man is anxious about (μεριμνᾷ) the things of the Lord, how he may please the Lord. But the married man is anxious about (μεριμνᾷ) the things of the world, how he may please his wife, and his attention is divided (καὶ μεμέρισται). And the unmarried woman and the virgin is anxious about (μεριμνᾷ) the things of the Lord so that she may be holy both

---

[38]Most commentators hold the two meanings of ἐνεστώς in tension. Barrett (1971, 175), for example, interprets ἡ ἐνεστῶσα ἀνάγκη as "the eschatological woes that are impending over the world, and are already anticipated in the sufferings of Christians." Conzelmann (1975, 132) resolves the tension by translating ἐνεστώς "imminent."

Recension q of 3 Maccabees refers to the desecration of the Temple by Antichus IV as ἡ ἐνεστῶσα ἀνάγκη (1:16). Interestingly, one of the responses to this distress is that women who have recently been married abandon the bridal chambers which have been prepared for marital relations (vv 18-19).

[39]See below p 113.

in body and in spirit. But the married woman is anxious about
(μεριμνᾳ) the things of the world, how she may please her
husband (πῶς ἀρεσῃ τῷ ἀνδρι).

Barrett raises a question about the interpretation of vv 32-35: Is Paul
criticizing the Corinthians who are advocating that believers should not
marry because they are too "anxious" in their efforts to please the Lord or
does he use "anxious" here in both a positive and a negative sense?[40] As
we shall see, Paul refuses to lay down absolute rules concerning marriage.
Thus, it is possible he is criticizing the Corinthians for creating anxiety by
making such rules and insisting that all follow them. More than likely,
however, Paul is using "being anxious about" in two different ways, just as
he had used "wisdom" in a number of ways in chapters 1-4. That is, he
contrasts being anxious about the things of the Lord to being anxious
about the things of the world. To be sure, as Barrett points out there are
difficulties with this interpretation, for since Paul acknowledges that
believers may marry, he cannot draw absolute distinctions between pleasing the Lord and pleasing one's mate. But, Paul himself appears to recognize the relative value of his argument, since in concluding it he indicates
that he offers this advice about remaining unmarried for the "benefit"
(σύμφορος) of the Corinthians and not to put a "noose" about their necks.
He is concerned with what is "fitting" (πρὸς τὸ εὔσχημον) and with what
contributes to their "waiting on the Lord with singlemindedness" (εὐπάρε-
δρον τῷ κυρίῳ ἀπερισπάστως, v 35).

V 35, therefore, is important for understanding Paul's argument against
marriage. It suggests that his objections are not to marriage in itself but
are purely functional. That is, "his argument is not a matter of what is
right or wrong, but of what is or is not expedient and profitable in particular circumstances."[41] And for Paul these "circumstances" are the end of
the age and the mission of believers. But since, as we shall see, Paul can
argue that the imminence of the end of this age is also a reason for
remaining unmarried, it would appear that he in fact attaches greater
significance to the argument regarding the mission of believers. This
becomes clearer in 1 Cor 9:5, where Paul argues that he and Barnabas
choose not to take wives with them on their missionary journeys so that
they may more freely devote themselves to the task of proclaiming the
gospel.

---

[40]1971, 178-179.
[41]Barrett 1971, 181.

Paul's functional approach to the question of whether believers should marry is therefore analogous to Epictetus' argument concerning the Ideal Cynic.[42] As we have seen, Epictetus did not claim that marriage in itself was wrong. Indeed, he argued that it was a civic duty which most men were obliged to perform for the survival of the city.[43] It was only for the Cynic who had taken up a divine mission that it was inappropriate, since he must devote himself freely to the performance of that mission.[44] Furthermore, one of the tasks of the mission was to insure that those who were married were properly fulfilling the obligations of married life.[45] Even Paul's eschatological argument has analogy in Epictetus' discourse on the Ideal Cynic in that the Cynic does not marry because the present order is "like a battlefield."[46] I point to these similarities between Paul and Epictetus not to claim that one was dependent on the other, but to demonstrate that since there were other groups in the Greco-Roman world with a strong sense of self-identity and a great concern with a mission to the larger world, Paul's argument against marriage would be readily understood by the Corinthians.[47]

There are of course other reasons for arguing that the Corinthians would not have found Paul's argument unusual, for as many scholars have noted, there are a striking number of similarities between Paul's terminology and that of the moralists. Epictetus and Antipater, for example, speak of the philosopher's being "free from distractions" (ἀπερισπά-στως).[48] Epictetus also recalls that Socrates, when urged by Crito to leave prison for the sake of his children, refused to do so, considering instead what was "fitting" (εὔσχημον) for the philosopher.[49] And Paul's

[42]See the discussion of Epictetus' discourse *On the Calling of a Cynic* in chapter 2, pp 42-43.
[43]3.7, 19-22.
[44]3.22,69.
[45]3.22,72.
[46]3.22,69.
[47]There is an important difference between Cynic and Christian self-identity in that only the latter was concerned with community. Although there were Cynic traditions, the Cynic street preachers appear to have been independent of one another. See Malherbe 1982, esp. 49-50 and 59: "In sum, Cynicism, which was essentially a way of life requiring no adherence to a canonical system of doctrine, continued to adapt itself to different viewpoints, and consequently retained the diversity which characterized it from early in its history."
[48]Epictetus 3.22,69; Antipater 256,34-257,4 von Arnim.
[49]4.1,163.

claim that married persons are "anxious about" (μεριμνᾷ) the things of the
world and about how to please (ἀρέσκειν) their mates echoes Menander's
observation that marriage has many "cares" (μερίμνας),[50] as well as the
Stoic and Neo-Pythagorean view of what was proper for a wife, namely,
"to please her husband" (ἀρέσκειν ἀνδρί).[51]

To limit comparison of Paul's arguments against marriage with those of
the Hellenistic world to specific terms common to both, however, does
not allow one to see just how much Paul was a part of the larger world.
Thus, when speaking of Paul's claim that marriage causes one to be
anxious, we must also recall that many in the Hellenistic world referred
to marriage as "a great struggle" (μέγας ἀγών),[52] as "burdensome and
grievous" (βάρος ἢ φορτίον),[53] and as "full of care" (φροντίδων πλέα).[54]
In these last examples the terminology is different but the basic argument
is the same: marriage distracts one from other obligations. Still, it must
be emphasized that, as with Epictetus, Paul's concern is *functional* and
not a rejection of marriage itself. It should also be stressed that, unlike
some of the other moralists (Theophrastus, for example),[55] Paul refers
only to the anxieties experienced by married persons. He does not refer to
women as a source of grief, which confirms that his primary concern is
with freeing believers to participate in the mission to which they are all
called, and should not be characterized as misogynist.

It is clear, therefore, that Paul prefers that unmarried persons—
whether single or widowed—remain as they are. Nevertheless, he is
unwilling to make his own preference an absolute rule. Indeed, in every
instance in which he advises the unmarried to remain as they are, he adds
that they are free to marry.

We see this from the very beginning of his counsel to the unmarried in
vv 8-9. Immediately after indicating that it is his wish that the unmarried
and widows remain as he himself is he adds, "But if they are not living
continently, let them marry, for it is better to marry than to burn." Paul
offers similar advice in vv 36-38: If a man's passions are strong (that is, if

---

[50]Stobaeus 4.517,13-14 Hense; K649.
[51]For the Stoics, see, for example, Antipater 255,22-23 von Arnim; for
the Neo-Pythagoreans, see the *Letter to Kleareta* 116,4-12 Thesleff.
[52]Antiphon, *On Harmony* 357,15-16 Diels.
[53]This is the opinion Hierocles rejects. See *On Marriage* 505,24-25
Hense.
[54]Antiphon, *On Harmony* 360, 1 Diels.
[55]On Theophrastus, see chapter 2, pp 35-36.

he *is* under compulsion, does *not* have his desires under control, and is *not* able to keep his virgin as she is), he should marry. In vv 28a and 39 he again states that the believer is free to marry, though in these verses he says nothing about the dangers of sexual immorality. In the former passage, having just advised that because of the imminent distress it is best to remain as one is and interpreting this to mean that those who are unmarried should remain unmarried, he adds that if a man or woman does marry they do not sin (ἐὰν δὲ καὶ γαμήσῃς, οὐχ ἥμαρτες, καὶ ἐὰν γήμῃ ἡ παρθένος, οὐχ ἥμαρτεν). And in the latter passage he says of the widow that although she will be happier if she remains unmarried, she is free to marry whomever she wishes. His only stipulation is that she should marry "only in the Lord" (ἐὰν δὲ κοιμηθῇ ὁ ἀνήρ, ἐλευθέρα ἐστὶν ᾧ θέλει γαμηθῆναι, μόνον ἐν κυρίῳ).

It is striking that the only reason Paul gives in favor of marriage is the danger of sexual immorality. We have already seen his concern with this issue in vv 2-6. Indeed, he begins his discussion of sexual intercourse within marriage "because of sexual immorality" and concludes it "lest Satan tempt you because of your incontinence." As we have seen, the two precepts Paul cites in v 2 linking the dangers of sexual immorality and marriage echo Jewish paraenetic tradition. But the avoidance of immorality is by no means the only reason for marrying in Jewish tradition. A man should marry, it maintained, in order to fulfill the divine command to "be fruitful and multiply."[56] Thus, Paul's concern with immorality alone is not in keeping with Jewish tradition. Paul's silence about marrying in order to produce children is even more profound in comparison with the Hellenistic *topos On Marriage,* especially given Paul's apparent familiarity with Hellenistic arguments against marriage.

As we saw in the survey of Hellenistic literature, the Stoics who addressed this *topos* argued specifically against those who held that marriage was a burden and prevented one from pursuing the philosophical way of life.[57] They claimed, for example, that marriage was "beneficial" (σύμφορος). Among the benefits accruing to married life were a wife, who took over the daily cares of running a household and thus allowed her husband to be "free from distraction" (ἀπερίσπαστος) for pursuing study and political affairs, and children, who were a help to parents when they are active and a source of comfort when they are old. By contrast, Paul advised the Corinthians that since the unmarried could serve the Lord

---

[56] On this requirement, see chapter 1, pp 21-22.
[57] See chapter 2, pp 32-41.

"free from distraction" (ἀπερισπάστως) his counseling them to remain unmarried was for their "benefit" (πρὸς τὸ ὑμῶν αὐτῶν σύμφορον). Moreover, he says nothing at all about producing children. As most commentators suggest, Paul did not refer to producing children in 1 Corinthians 7 because he expected the end of the age imminently. But in view of the Stoic discussion of marriage and producing children we can perhaps say more than this. In the first place, the Stoics argued that one should marry and produce children not simply because to do so was beneficial, but also because it was a matter of obligation (τῶν ἀναγκαιοτάτων καὶ πρώτων καθηκόντων).[58] That is, producing children was the means of insuring the survival of the city. But for Paul and his followers this was scarcely a matter of prime importance. Indeed, Stoics themselves would not have bothered with advising many of Paul's converts to produce children, for their primary concern was with citizens, not with the mass of slaves, tradesmen, and even freedmen who made up the population of a city.[59] Thus, it is not surprising Paul does not take up this aspect of the Stoic arguments. Furthermore, since Paul argued that it was beneficial for believers to remain unmarried because it allowed them to be free from distraction for the service of the Lord, he would not have seen a wife and children as beneficial. Moreover, Paul was concerned that wives as well as husbands be free from distraction, since they too were called into the Lord's service. Thus, it would appear that Paul's silence about children and the benefits of married life was due not simply to the imminence of the end of the age, but also to the inappropriateness of most of the common arguments in favor of being married and producing children.

If Paul is silent with respect to the common arguments in favor of marriage and producing children, the moralists are likewise silent about marrying to avoid sexual immorality. The closest one comes to this

---

[58]The quotation is from Antipater On Marriage 255,5 von Arnim. See the discussion in chapter 2, pp 41-44.

[59]Antipater, for example, addresses the "well-born" (εὐγενής), courageous (εὔψυχος) youth who is cultured (ἥμερος) and civic-minded (πολιτικός)," (On Marriage 254,25 von Arnim). By contrast there are few in the Corinthian community who are wise, powerful, and well-born (1 Cor 1:26). This is not to say, however, that all in the community were of low social status. The prosopographic evidence suggests that Pauline Christianity attracted those with wealth and social status as well as the socially disadvantaged. For a discussion of the evidence and a review of recent literature on this subject, see Meeks 1983, chapter 2.

argument is Antipater's criticism of his contemporaries who neglect marriage and its obligations because of their "inclination to sexual pleasure
and the easy life" (ἡ ἐπὶ τὸ καταφερὲς καὶ ῥάθυμον ἐπίκλισις).[60]

There is one feature of the Hellenistic moralists' treatment of marriage that Paul does share: the concern with whom one should marry. But
even here Paul's interests are not those of most of the moralists. As we
have seen, the moralists pay great attention to the question of whom one
should marry. They advise one not to marry for wealth, noble birth, or for
beauty. They even give specific instructions on how to learn of a woman's
character. One should observe her parents and make inquiries of the
household servants and the tradespeople who frequent the house.[61] Paul's
advice about choosing a marriage partner is not directed to these issues,
however, but to group boundaries. He addresses this in his advice to
widows in v 39-40. He says of the widow that she is free to marry, but
adds the stipulation "only in the Lord" (μόνον ἐν κυρίῳ). Even if one
follows Lightfoot and argues that this phrase does not mean "only in the
circle of believers" but " [remembering] that she is a member of Christ's
body; and not [forgetting] her Christian duties and responsibilities,"[62] it is
difficult to imagine Paul's not preferring that the widow marry a believer.
Thus, the least one can say is that her being a believer determines her
choice of a partner. More than likely, however, "only in the Lord" does
mean that the person the widow chooses should be a fellow believer.[63]

Even here, however, Paul's advice was not without analogy in the
Hellenistic world, for the moralists argued that a man should choose
someone like himself as a wife. For the most part, though, their concern
was limited to the woman's social status. The wife should be neither below
nor above her husband. Again, however, it is the Cynics who were closest
to Paul, for they too maintained that a wife should hold beliefs similar to
those of her husband and follow the Cynic way of life along with him. We
saw this, for example, in Epictetus' reference to the marriage of Crates
and Hipparchia and in the Cynic letters attributed to Crates.[64] This issue

---

[60] *On Marriage* 255,31-34 von Arnim.

[61] See chapter 2, p 47.

[62] 1895, 235.

[63] Note that in 1 Cor 9:5 Paul speaks of "a sister as wife" (ἀδελφὴ
γυνή).

[64] See chapter 2, pp 52-53.

is important to the Cynic because, like the early Christians, they were very conscious of their own identity.[65] Unlike Paul's arguments against marriage, therefore, his argument in favor of it would have sounded unusual to the Corinthians. Indeed, it may well have struck them as being rather weak. Scholars are sharply divided over how to interpret Paul's argument in favor of marriage. Some argue that his admission that some should marry is indeed a grudging admission, since he allows marriage *only* as a remedy for incontinence. Most, however, point out that because Paul's treatment of marriage in 1 Corinthians 7 is not systematic, but directed to a specific situation, it is not legitimate to conclude that the danger of sexual immorality would have been the only reason he might otherwise have given in favor of marrying. But if, as I have suggested, the common arguments in favor of marriage dealt with issues which were foreign to Paul and his followers, his failure to list other reasons for marrying is perhaps less striking. Still, since Paul knew of husbands and wives who worked together in trade and in mission (among whom were Prisca and Acquila, who sent greetings to Corinth [16:19]), it is noteworthy that Paul does not use them as an example of "successful" marriage.

In the final analysis, therefore, we can only say that Paul's clear preference is for unmarried believers to remain single. But he never makes this a rule. For in every instance in which he expresses this opinion, he adds that the unmarried are free to marry. Moreover, his objections were not to marriage itself and still less to women as a group. He is concerned primarily that all believers—both men and women—be free to serve the Lord with single-mindedness.

ADVICE TO THOSE WHO ARE MARRIED

Alongside his discussion of whether believers should marry Paul addresses himself to those who are already married. We have seen this in vv 2-6, where Paul deals with the question of sexual intercourse between married persons. In v 10 Paul turns to another issue of concern to those who are married: divorce. In the first instance he addresses couples in which both partners are believers. In telling them not to seek a divorce he makes it clear that the rule he cites is not his own but the Lord's (παραγγέλλω, οὐκ ἐγὼ ἀλλὰ ὁ κύριος). Interestingly, the form of the

---

[65]Again, however, as individuals and not as a community. See n 46 above.

saying he gives here is closer to the Marcan form, in that it admits of no extenuating circumstances.[66] Nevertheless, Paul adds (specifically to the wife, but presumably applicable to the husband as well), "but if you do divorce, let the woman remain unmarried or be reconciled to her husband."[67]

Next, in vv 12-16, Paul addresses believers who are married to nonbelievers. Here the advice Paul gives is his own, since he had no word from the Lord dealing with this situation.[68] His advice, however, is fundamentally the same as that for believing couples: Do not seek a divorce—as long as the choice is yours. But, he adds, if the non-believing partner desires separation, the believer should not resist. This much of vv 12-16 is clear enough. Paul's attempt to justify his claim that believers should not seek separation from their non-believing partners, however, contains a number of vexing problems.[69] Without attempting to unravel all of them, we may note that the presupposition of Paul's argument (explicit in v 14) is that the children of mixed marriages are holy,

---

[66]Against Dungan 1971, 131.

[67] Murphy-O'Connor (1981), who emphasizes that χωρισθῆναι is passive, suggests that, in keeping with Paul's usage in 1 Cor 6:7 and Rom 12:2, v 10b should be translated "the wife should not allow herself to be separated from her husband" and thus reflects Jewish rather than Greco-Roman law. He argues further that since Paul addresses the woman rather than the man (in contrast to the dominical sayings), Paul must have had a specific case in mind, one in which the husband wished to follow the ascetic ideal expressed in the Corinthians' slogan in v 1b while the wife continued to insist on her conjugal rights. There is nothing in the Jewish texts dealing with divorce, however, to suggest that the woman had any right to allow or disallow a divorce. The decision rested solely with the husband. Furthermore, Paul's concern with balancing statements addressed to men and women (on which see below) and the situation Paul deals with in 1 Cor 11:2-16 (in which women have sought to remove all signs of distinction between men and women in the exercise of the gift of prophecy) suggest that it may well have been women rather than men who were withdrawing from sexual relations within marriage. This too would explain why Paul addresses women first in vv 10-11.

Murphy-O'Connor is correct, however, in pointing out (against Elliott 1983) that ἀφιέναι and χωρίζειν both mean divorce in vv 10-11 and vv 12-16. See the literature cited by Fitzmyer (1976, 211).

[68]That is, the dominical saying Paul cites in v 10 presupposes that both partners are Jews.

[69]Most notable is the question of how the sanctification of the nonbelieving spouse is effected.

presumably because of the believing parent. With this the Corinthians apparently agree. But Paul infers from the holiness of the children that the believing partner also sanctifies the non-believing partner, because otherwise (ἐπεὶ ἄρα) the children would also be unholy (lit. "unclean"). That is, what the believing partner accomplishes for the child he also accomplishes for the non-believing spouse. V 16 makes clear, however, that Paul does not mean here that in being sanctified by the believing partner the non-believer is made a member of the community. The salvation of the non-believing partner remains an open question. He means, rather, that the holiness of the believing partner is sufficient to insure that the marriage itself is holy and therefore need not be dissolved.

V 16 raises another set of problems. Is it to be taken directly with v 15 or as referring back to vv 12-14? That is, does it express resignation in view of the non-believer's desire to separate ("Do not resist your partner's wishes, since after all you have no way of knowing whether you can effect his salvation") or does it reflect the concerns of mission ("Do not seek divorce from your non-believing spouse, since there is always the possibility that you may win him")? If one were to translate the last phrase of v 15 "For God has called you to peace" (with, for example, the RSV),[70] v 16 would appear to be an expression of resignation. But since Paul in fact says "But God has called you to peace," it is better to take v 16 (and indeed v 15b) in contrast to v 15a and therefore as another reason not to separate from a non-believing spouse. In support of this reading Johannes Weiss points to 1 Cor 9:19-22 where Paul uses σώσω synonymously with the missionary term κερδήσω.[71] In further support of this reading Joachim Jeremias had demonstrated that there is good linguistic evidence for translating εἰ as "perhaps" when it occurs with the indicative following verbs meaning "to know."[72] Thus, for Paul the hope of winning one's non-believing spouse is another reason for remaining married to him or her.

Finally, it is worth noting that Paul's advice in vv 12-16 is in keeping with his views in 5:9-13. The believer, that is, is not to seek complete separation from the world. This observation is especially important if, as may well be the case, Paul's concern in vv 10-16 is with some of the

---

[70]The RSV actually reads "For God has called us to peace." But ὑμᾶς is to be preferred.
[71]1910, 183.
[72]1954, 255-260.

rigorists in Corinth who were advocating divorce in order to avoid all sexual immorality.[73]

We saw above that one of the conclusions Paul drew from his belief in the imminent end of the age was that those who are unmarried should not seek to be married. We must now qualify this observation by noting that Paul in fact argued that because the end of the age was at hand, one should remain as one is—whether married or single. That is, "Are you bound to a wife? Do not seek to be loosed. Are you free from a wife? Do not seek one."[74] Then in v 29 he speaks further of the significance of the imminent end of the age for married persons: Since the time has been shortened and the form of this world is passing away, "those who have wives should live as if they did not" (οἱ ἔχοντες γυναῖκας ὡς μὴ ἔχοντες ὦσιν). As Barrett observes, vv 2-5 clearly rule out taking this to mean that married persons should abstain from sexual intercourse. It means, rather, that just as those who buy should do so as if they were not entering into possession of what they have bought, and just as those who use the world should do so without being taken over by it, so those who are married should not be restricted by the demands of married life, but treat it as it actually is—part of the world which is passing away.[75]

In every instance in which Paul addresses married persons, therefore, his advice is "Do not seek to end your marriage." This absolute rejection of divorce is the one area in which Paul is clearly unlike all of his contemporaries. Both Jewish and Greco-Roman law provided for divorce with few restrictions. And, as we have seen, it was very common, especially in Greco-Roman circles.[76] Even the Stoics, who advocated marriage so vigorously, say nothing against it. The closest one comes to Paul's view is the Neo-Pythagorean admonition to women not to divorce their unfaithful husbands since this is precisely what their rivals would like to happen.[77] Very likely, Paul's absolute rejection of divorce derives from the dominical saying he cites in v 10. Thus, although Paul did not take this saying legalistically (as vv 11 and 15 indicate), he did see it as binding on believers in such a way as to distinguish their practice from that of the world around them.

---

[73]See below pp 117-122.

[74]So also Robertson-Plummer (1914, 150), Heinrici (1888, 213), Moffatt (1954, 91), and Baltensweiler (1976, 170).

[75]1971, 176-177.

[76]See chapter 2, p 63.

[77]See, for example, Theano's letter *To Euridice* 197, 12-24 Thesleff. Plutarch gives similar counsel in *Advice* 40 (*Moralia* 140A).

So far we have seen that although Paul advised those who are not married to remain single because of the imminent distress and because the unmarried can more readily give their undivided attention to the service of the Lord, he says that in fact they should marry if they are unable to control their sexual desires. We have also seen that he encourages those who are married to remain married as long as the decision was theirs and that here, too, the imminent distress was a factor. We must now consider one final aspect of his response to the Corinthians' inquiries concerning sexual matters, one which has immediate bearing on our understanding of his use of traditional rules: his concern with both men and women.

PAUL'S CONCERN WITH MEN AND WOMEN

Perhaps with most striking difference between Paul's formulation of the precepts in 1 Thess 4:3b-4 and in 1 Cor 7:2 is his inclusion of advice to wives: "Let each man have his own wife and let each woman have her own husband" (ἕκαστος τὴν ἑαυτοῦ γυναῖκα ἐχέτω καὶ ἑκάστη τὸν ἴδιον ἄνδρα ἐχέτω). This balancing of concern with men and women is all the more pronounced because Paul employs it throughout 1 Corinthians 7,[78] as the following list indicates:

The husband should give to his wife her conjugal rights, and likewise (ὁμοίως δὲ καὶ) the wife to her husband (v 3).

For the wife does not rule over her own body, her husband does; likewise (ὁμοίως δὲ καὶ) the husband does not rule over his own body, his wife does (v 4).

The wife should not separate (μὴ χωρισθῆναι) from her husband . . . and the husband should not divorce (μὴ ἀφιέναι) his wife (v 10).

If any brother has a wife who is an unbeliever, and she consents to live with him, he should not divorce (μὴ ἀφιέτω) her. And if any woman has a husband who is an unbeliever, and he consents to live with her, she should not divorce (μὴ ἀφιέτω) him. For the unbelieving husband is sanctified through his

---

[78]This has been pointed out by Meeks 1974, 199-200 and Scroggs 1972, 294-295. See the qualifications made to Scroggs' interpretation of the evidence in Pagels 1974.

wife, and the unbelieving wife is sanctified through her husband (vv 12-14).

Wife, how do you know whether you will save your husband? Husband, how to you know whether you will save your wife? (v 16)?

In v 27 Paul departs from this balanced structure somewhat when he addresses men only, "Are you bound to a wife? Do not seek to be free. Are you free from a wife? Do not seek a wife." But in v 28 he returns to it by adding, "But if you do marry, you do not sin, and if the virgin (ἡ παρθένος) marries she does not sin." Similarly, in v 29 he refers to husbands only when he charges, "Let those who have wives live as though they did not." But again, when discussing further the worldly cares against which the advice on living "as if not" contends, he observes:

> The unmarried man is anxious about the affairs of the Lord, how to please the Lord; but the married man is anxious about worldly affairs, how to please his wife . . . And the unmarried woman or girl is anxious about the affairs of the Lord, how to be holy in body and spirit; but the married woman is anxious about worldly affairs, how to please her husband (vv 32-34).

Significantly, Paul shows this same concern with balancing his treatment of men and women in 11:2-16, a section dealing with worship in the Corinthian community. To be sure, v 3 implies the subordination of women to men. But as Wayne Meeks points out, Paul is in fact concerned that both men *and* women be properly attired when exercising their prophetic gifts.[79] That is, it is as inappropriate for a man to prophesy with his head covered as it is for a woman to prophesy with her head uncovered. Thus, Paul never claims that a woman should not prophesy in the assembly. Here, as throughout his discussion of worship (11:2-14:40) Paul is concerned, rather, that all be done "seemly and with order" (εὐσχημόνως καὶ κατὰ τάξιν, 14:40).

In a very suggestive analysis of this passage Elisabeth Schüssler Fiorenza has demonstrated why Paul was so concerned with seemliness and order.[80] Noting that in v 15 Paul claims that a woman's *hair* was

---

[79] 1974, 201.
[80] 1983, 226-235. Walker (1975) and Cope (1978) and Trompf (1980) have argued that 1 Cor 11:2-16 is an interpolation. Walker repeats this claim in

given to her "for a covering" (ἀντὶ περιβολαίου), Schüssler Fiorenza rejects the common view that Paul seeks to impose the Jewish custom of wearing a veil. Instead, she argues, Paul was warning against the woman's wearing her hair unbound and flowing loosely, a practice common among women in the cults of Dionysos, Cybele, Pythia, and the Sibyl. In these cults "unbound hair was necessary for a woman to produce an effective magical incantation" and thus was "a mark of true prophecy."[81] Paul, therefore, warns against this practice so that the worship of the Corinthian community may not be identified with the orgiastic worship of the cults. Again, however, Paul does not claim that women should not prophesy; he argues, rather, that they should do so, in a manner that is "seemly and in order."

Indeed, in vv 11-12 Paul again emphasizes the equality of men and women. V 11 is usually translated, "Nevertheless, in the Lord woman is not independent of man nor man of woman." But Schüssler Fiorenza claims that χωρίς more frequently means not "independent of" or "without" but "different from," "unlike," "otherwise," "heterogeneous," or "of another kind."[82] Thus, she translates v 11, "In the Lord woman is not different from man nor man from woman." This view of the equality of men and women, Paul argues, is in fact in keeping with the created order: "For as woman [was created] from man, so man [is born] from woman, but both (lit. all) are from God."

Compared with Jewish paraenesis and with most paraenetic traditions in the Greco-Roman world, Paul's careful balancing of advice to men and women is unusual.[83] As we have seen, however, it does have analogy in

---

his most recent article on this passage (1983), citing a number of unpublished papers in support of it. He concludes, "I fully expect that this view will gain increasing acceptance by scholars in the field of New Testament studies" (109 n 21). Like Schüssler Fiorenza (1983, 230), however, I am skeptical about the search for interpolations.

[81] 277. Lösch (1947) offers a similar interpretation. See also Murphy-O'Connor 1980, though he treats the problem as one in which both men and women are wearing their hair in ways untypical of their sex rather than one dealing with cultic matters.

[82] 1983, 229. In this she follows Kürzinger 1978, 270-275. Murphy-O'Connor (1980, 497 n 60) also follows Kürzinger in this reading of χωρίς.

[83] Meeks (1974, 199-200) observes, "Thus Paul presupposes and approves in the Corinthian congregation an equivalence of role and a mutuality of relationship between the sexes in matters of marriages, divorce, and charismatic leadership of the church to a degree that is virtually unparalleled in Jewish or pagan society of the time." This view is not without its detractors, however. See Pagels 1974 and Schüssler Fiorenza 1983.

the Stoic tradition. The parallels are most clearly seen in Musonius' diatribes *That Women Too Should Study Philosophy* and *Should Daughters Receive the Same Education as Sons?* In the latter, for example, Musonius argues that since "understanding" (φρονεῖν), "living justly" (δικαίως βιοῦν), "courage" (ἀνδρεία), and indeed all the virtues are just as important for women as for men, daughters should in fact receive the same education as sons.[84] With regard to marriage specifically, we should recall that in discussing whether marriage is a handicap for the pursuit of philosophy Musonius asked, "To whom is everything judged to be common, body, soul, and possessions except man and wife?"[85] Similarly, Musonius claimed that fidelity in sexual relations was just as important for husbands as for wives.[86] Here again, therefore, the advice Paul gives was consonant with advice the Corinthians may have heard in other contexts. The one distinction in Paul's advice is that the equality of men and women derives primarily from their being "in the Lord" (1 Cor 11:11 and Gal 3:28).

Having now examined Paul's response to the Corinthians' letter, we may now turn to the question raised at the beginning of this chapter: Why does Paul reformulate the tradition he cited in 1 Thessalonians 4? To answer this question we must examine the situation at Corinth and the issues raised in the letter the Corinthians sent to Paul.

THE SITUATION AT CORINTH WHICH DEMANDS THE REFORMULATION OF TRADITION

The situation Paul faced in Corinth was extremely complex. Indeed, the details of it continue to intrigue New Testament scholars. Fortunately, however, there is general agreement now concerning its basic elements and we may use this consensus as the basis of our analysis of Paul's reformulation of tradition. According to the *communis opinio* (1) there were some in the Corinthian community who claimed that they had already experienced the resurrection; and (2) the individual problems Paul deals

---

[84] 44,9-46,2 Lutz.
[85] *Is Marriage a Handicap?* 94, 8-11 Lutz.
[86] *Should Daughters Receive the Same Education?* 44, 16-18 Lutz.

with in 1 Corinthians were somehow related to this belief.[87] To what
extent does this analysis of the situation at Corinth help us in determining
the nature of the problem dealing with sexual immorality? Before
addressing this question directly, it will be helpful to examine briefly two
of the other problems Paul encounters so that we may be clear in understanding the issues at stake—at least as far as Paul is concerned. These
problems are the claim to superior knowledge and the dispute over spiritual gifts.

Paul treats the problem stemming from the claim to superior knowledge in chapters 1-4 and 8:1-11:1. In 1-3 he takes great pains to show that
the claim to superior wisdom is a false one and leads to divisions in the
community.[88] He argues that since God had destroyed the wisdom of this
age, he himself had not proclaimed the gospel with eloquent wisdom, "lest
the cross of Christ be emptied of its power" and that since the wisdom he
does proclaim comes to believers as the gift of God, there are no grounds
for boasting in it. He adds, moreover, that the divisions that have resulted
from the claim to superior wisdom indicate that the Corinthians are
immature in their faith and consequently unable to receive the solid food
which is reserved for those who are spiritually mature.

In 8:1-11:1 the claim to special knowledge is also at issue and again its
result is division in the community. Those who claimed to know that "an
idol has no real existence" and that "there is no God but one" appear to
have been setting themselves above those who lacked this knowledge and
whose conscience, being weak, was defiled by the practice of eating meat
sacrificed to idols. Paul agrees with the "strong": Idols do not have any
real existence and there is no God but one. Nevertheless, he argues that
those who have this knowledge should not insist on their rights but consider their weaker brothers. For "'knowledge' puffs up, but love builds
up."

The dispute over spiritual gifts is reflected in chapters 12-14. The
primary issue here is "glossolalia," speaking in tongues. Glossolalia
appears to have been highly valued by the Corinthian community and
regarded by some as the gift of the spirit *par excellence*. Indeed, as
Wayne Meeks observes, "we might well guess that trance experiences of

---

[87]See Käsemann 1960, 1962; Boers 1967; Wilson 1968; Koester 1961;
Funk 1966, 277-305; Dahl 1977, 40-61; Horsley 1978 and Thiselton 1977.
[88]On chapters 1-4 see Wilckens 1959 together with the critical reviews
of Koester (1961) and Funk (1966, 277-305).

the sort that produce glossolalia *could* have served as strong reinforcement of [the Corinthians' belief that they had already experienced the resurrection]."[89] But not all in the community possessed the gift of glossolalia. Consequently those who were adept in it apparently considered themselves superior to those who were not. Again, therefore, the claim to superiority leads to divisions within the community. In responding to this situation Paul can claim that he himself speaks in tongues more than any of the Corinthians. He points out, however, that glossolalia is not the most important of the gifts of the spirit. It is better, he argues, to seek the "higher gifts," chief among which is prophecy. For while prophecy itself builds up the community, speaking in tongues builds up the community only if there is someone present to interpret what is being said.[90]

In chapters 1-4, 8:1-11:1, and 12-14, therefore, Paul addresses himself to situations in which one group within the Corinthian community is claiming superiority over another, on the one hand because of their claim to superior knowledge and on the other because of their boasting in their ability to speak in tongues. In both instances, Paul's greatest concern is with the resulting division in the community.

In chapter 7 Paul is faced with a similar situation. That is, those who are claiming that "it is good for a man not to touch a woman" regard abstinence from all sexual intercourse as a sign of participation in the resurrection, have made abstinence the standard of behavior for all believers, and look down on those who are unable to live up to it. Again, the result is division in the community—not between libertines and ascetics, however, but between ascetics and those who would continue normal sexual relations within marriage.

To be sure, we have no explicit evidence that the Corinthians were claiming that abstinence from sexual intercourse was a sign of participation in the resurrection. But such a rigorous view is in keeping with their claim to superior knowledge and the emphasis on speaking in tongues. All three, that is, would serve to distinguish "spiritual" people from the "unspiritual."

We know from 5:9-13 that there were some in Corinth who interpreted Paul's earlier letter to mean that they should separate themselves completely from the "immoral" of the outside world. More to the point here, however, is that the question of marriage and sexual intercourse had

---

[89] 1983, 121.

[90] On the importance of "building up" in chapters 12-14, see Bornkamm 1969, 161-169.

created a division *within* the community and that the group which argued
vigorously against both apparently maintained that their slogan "it is good
for a man not to touch a woman" applied even to those who were married.
Indeed, it appears likely that this group held that if married persons were
unable to abstain from sexual relations they should divorce. For as J.C.
Hurd has observed, while "it is difficult to see how Paul's emphatic rejection of divorce in 1 Cor 7:10,11 could be considered an extension of his
argument in 7:1-9 . . . certainly divorce could be justified by [the Corinthians'] slogan as quoted by Paul."[91] Thus, not content with distinguishing
themselves from outsiders, the rigorists also distinguished themselves
from those in the community who were unable to uphold their "higher"
standards. Such spiritual elitism with regard to marriage and sexual
intercourse would at least be in keeping with the elitism which obtained
in the dispute over speaking in tongues and the claim to superior knowledge.

Paul's argument concerning differing gifts in 7:7 is further evidence
that the question of marriage and sexual intercourse is related to the
dispute over speaking in tongues. For even if the Corinthians were not
claiming that celibacy was the gift of God (and it is tempting to say that
they were), Paul's arguing that not all have this gift suggests that he sees
the debate concerning marriage and sexual intercourse in terms of spiritual gifts. Thus, just as he checks the spiritual elitism which grows out of
the Corinthians' emphasis on speaking in tongues by insisting that there is
a diversity of gifts, so he counters the claim that all should be celibate by
pointing out that while some do have this gift, others have gifts of a
different nature. Therefore, to the extent that the claim to superior
knowledge and the emphasis on speaking in tongues reinforces the Corinthians' belief that they had already experienced the resurrection, their
ability to abstain from all sexual relations does as well.

Still, it is appropriate to ask how the Corinthians could have come to
the conclusion that "spiritual" people should abstain from all sexual intercourse, especially since such a view was against the practice of both
Jewish and Greco-Roman culture. The answer to this probably lies in Paul
himself. We have seen that the paraenetic tradition Paul used in his
baptismal instruction in Thessalonica advised believers to marry "in
holiness and honor not in the passion of desire, as the Gentiles who do not
know God." Although we have no explicit evidence that Paul cited this
precept in his teaching in Corinth also, it is probable that he did, since his

---

[91]1965, 167.

baptismal instruction doubtless took much the same form in every city. If he did stress that one must marry in holiness and honor, it is not hard to imagine rigorists interpreting this to mean that it is better to avoid the passion of desire completely. After all, they could point to Paul (their father in the faith [1 Cor 4:14-15]) as an example, for unlike the other apostles who traveled from place to place preaching the gospel, he and Barnabas were not accompanied by wives. Indeed, when discussing the problem of meat sacrificed to idols Paul refers to their traveling without wives as an example of foregoing one's rights (1 Cor 9:5). Furthermore, in 7:7 and 8 Paul even expresses the desire that all live with respect to marriage as he himself does. Again, that is, just as Paul agrees with those who have no objection to eating meat sacrificed to idols and just as he agrees that speaking in tongues has value (and in fact speaks in tongues more than any of the Corinthians), so he agrees that it is better for believers not to marry.

In all probability, therefore, the Corinthians derived their position from Paul himself. This is not to say, however, that the Corinthians were able to quote Paul directly that "it is good for a man not to touch a woman." For if Paul's preference for remaining single had been clearly expressed either in his baptismal paraenesis or in an earlier letter, it is impossible to see how the issue could have arisen as it did.[92] It is more likely, rather, that the Corinthians themselves developed this view in the same way they came to emphasize their speaking in tongues and boast in their superior knowledge—to give expression to their view of themselves as participants in the resurrection and to demonstrate that they were spiritually superior to the rest of the believers in the community.

If this analysis of the situation in Corinth is correct, it would appear that Paul reformulates the tradition precisely because some of the Corinthians have interpreted it in a way he cannot accept. They have taken his warning concerning sexual immorality and the passion of desire as a call to abstain from all sexual intercourse and made abstinence the rule for everyone. To the extent that the Corinthians' slogan forbids incestuous

---

[92]Hurd (1965, chapters 6 and 8) argues that in Paul's earliest preaching he had advocated that "it is good for a man not to touch a woman" (though he considers 7:1b as a quotation from the Corinthians' letter) and that after the Apostolic Council he altered his view to accord with the decree which grew out of the council. He concludes, therefore, that the Corinthians' confusion over the question of marriage is the result of Paul's change of opinion. This aspect of Hurd's reconstruction, however, is not convincing. See the criticisms of Barrett (1971, 6-8).

relations or intercourse with prostitutes, Paul can agree with it. He himself clearly forbids both. To the extent that the slogan requires abstinence from intercourse within marriage or even prohibits marriage itself, however, he cannot agree with it. For he recognizes that all do not have the gift of celibacy. That is, he rejects the Corinthians' attempt to make one expression of the spiritual life binding on all believers, since to claim that there is only one legitimate expression of the spirit leads to elitism, which in turn leads to divisions in the community.

Conclusion

Our analysis of Paul's treatment of marriage is now complete. We have observed Paul at work not as a systematic theologian reflecting on moral issues while detached from the day-to-day struggles of average believers, but as a missionary-pastor wrestling with the problems of small house churches composed of recent converts to a new faith.

This is not to say that Paul had no theological concerns. Clearly he did. For in 1 Thessalonians 4 and 1 Corinthians 7 Paul grounds his discussion of marriage and sexual morality in theological reflection. Indeed, when one compares the precepts he rehearses with those of the Greco-Roman moralists and discovers just how similar they were, the theological element in his treatment stands out sharply. As we saw, for Paul one abstains from "the passion of desire" not because "reason" demands it or because it contributes to the development of one's character. One avoids the passion of desire because to do so is God's will, is pleasing to the Lord, and is in keeping with the precepts given in the name of the Lord Jesus. Similarly, when Paul addresses the questions raised by the Corinthians, his discussion reflects arguments employed in the moralists' debate over whether the wise man should marry. But when Paul adopts these arguments he is not concerned with the pursuit of philosophy or the survival of the city, but with "pleasing the Lord" and participating in mission. Thus, in supporting his position he cites the words of the Lord and the commandments of God. Moreover, even when Paul has no word from the Lord he claims that he speaks as one who "by the Lord's mercy is trustworthy," as one who "has the Spirit of God."

One can also discuss Paul's eschatological justification of the precepts regarding marriage and sexual morality under the rubric of theology. After all, while in the Greco-Roman world cases involving adultery could be brought to civic authorities, for Paul it is God who is the "avenging judge" in such matters. Furthermore, since the form of this world is passing away and since the appointed time has grown short, for Paul the values by which one should live are not the values of the world, but those of the world to come. This means, as far as marriage is concerned, that married persons should live as if they were not married.

Clearly, therefore, the theological element in Paul's treatment of marriage and sexual morality is important. But herein lies the irony, for in spite of the similarity between Paul's treatment of marriage and that of the Hellenistic moralists, Paul claims that to follow the precepts he gives distinguishes believers from "the Gentiles who do not know God."

As we saw, however, in 1 Thess 4:3-8, where Paul makes this claim most explicitly, he appears to be following Jewish traditions which had already incorporated material from the Hellenistic moralists and adapted it to meet the needs of Jews living in the diaspora. Paul not only adopts these traditions, he also uses them to the same effect—to distinguish believers from non-believers and thereby encourage them to continue in their new faith. In 1 Thessalonians 4, therefore, the precepts on marriage and sexual morality are to be read as polemic and not as objective description of social reality. This suggests that Paul was not dealing with specific moral problems in Thessalonica but cites precepts regarding marriage and sexual morality with a view to general exhortation.

The situation in Corinth was quite different. Here Paul was dealing with specific problems. But again, I suggest that sexual immorality was not one of the problems, at least in 1 Corinthians 7. Instead, the problem concerned one group's creating division in the community by claiming that "it is good for a man not to touch a woman" and looking down on those who were unable to live up to this standard. This ascetic elitism was one expression (along with speaking in tongues, eating meat sacrificed to idols, and claiming special knowledge) of the rigorists' belief that they had already experienced the resurrection and were consequently superior to those outside the community and to those within it who did not possess these spiritual gifts. In response to this situation, Paul returns to the traditional precepts, this time, however, citing them in more direct language and adding to them a discussion of whether believers should marry. His sympathies are with the rigorists, but he chastizes them for imposing their views on everyone in the community and thereby causing division within it. The solidarity of the community, he argues, is more important than the means of distinguishing it. Distinguishing believers, that is, should never result in dividing them.

By inquiring into the function of Paul's precepts on marriage and sexual morality and the purpose of his discussion of whether believers should marry, we have been able to shift the focus of the debate over Paul's reputedly negative view of marriage and to avoid entanglement in the attempts to analyze his psychological makeup that have grown out of this debate. We have seen that while Paul did prefer that believers remain unmarried, it was not because he regarded sexual intercourse as inherently evil or because he had no appreciation of married life. His concern lies elsewhere. Paul's approach, like that of Epictetus, was essentially practical. Believers, like the Ideal Cynic, should be able to devote themselves completely to the service of God. But for Paul serving God was not an individual affair. It was a matter of community. Thus, he speaks even more strongly when addressing those who divide the community by demanding that believers abstain from all sexual relations than he does when expressing his own views regarding marriage.

In sum, Paul's treatment of marriage is in keeping with his ethics as a whole. Whether one marries or remains single, one must live in a way that is pleasing to God and builds up the community of God's people.

Bibliography

TEXTS AND TRANSLATIONS OF
INDIVIDUAL AUTHORS

Achilles Tatius. *Clitophon and Leucippe*. 2nd ed. Trans. S. Gaselee. LCL. Cambridge: Harvard University Press.

Alciphron. *The Letters*. Trans. A. R. Benner and F. H. Fobes. LCL. Cambridge: Harvard University Press.

Aphthonius. "The Progymnasmata of Aphthonius in Translation." Trans. R. Nadeau. *Speech Monographs* 19 (1952), 264-285.

Aristotle. *Nicomachean Ethics*. Trans. H. Rackham. LCL. Cambridge: Harvard University Press.

_____. *Politics*. Trans. H. Rackham. LCL. Cambridge: Harvard University Press.

Pseudo-Aristotle. *Oeconomica and Magna Moralia*. Trans. G. C. Armstrong. LCL. Cambridge: Harvard University Press.

Athenaeus. *Deipnosophists*. 7 vols. Trans. C. B. Gulick. LCL. Cambridge: Harvard University Press.

Aulus Gellius. *Attic Nights*. 3 vols. Trans. J. C. Rolfe. LCL. Cambridge: Harvard University Press.

The Babylonian Talmud. Ed. Isodore Epstein. London: Soncino, 1935-1948.

Biblia Hebraica. 16th ed. Rudolf Kittel, Albrecht Alt, and Otto Eissfeldt. Stüttgart: Württembergische Bibelanstalt, 1973.

Bryson. *Der Oikonomikos des Neupythagoreers 'Bryson' und sein Einfluss auf die islamische Wissenschaft. Edition und Übersetzung der erhaltenen Versionen*. Ed. and trans. M. Plessner. Orient und Antike 5. Heidelberg: Winter, 1928.

Catullus. *Poems.* Trans. F. W. Cornish. LCL. Cambridge: Harvard University Press.

Columella. *On Agriculture.* 3 vols. Trans. H. B. Ash. LCL. Cambridge: Harvard University Press.

Pseudo-Clemens Romanus. *Die Pseudoklementinen.* Ed. B. Rehm. GCS. Berlin: Akademie, 1965.

_____. *Recognitions of Clement.* Trans. Thomas Smith. In *Ante-Nicene Fathers* 8. Reprint. Grand Rapids: Eerdmans, 1978.

Dio Cassius. *Roman History.* 9 vols. Trans. E. Cary. LCL. Cambridge: Harvard University Press.

Dio Chrysostom. *Orations.* 5 vols. Trans. J. W. Cohoon and H. L. Crosby. LCL. Cambridge: Harvard University Press.

Diodorus Siculus. *Library of History.* 12 vols. Trans. C. H. Oldfather et al. LCL. Cambridge: Harvard University Press.

Diogenes Laertius. *Lives and Opinions of Eminent Philosophers.* 2 vols. Trans. R. D. Hicks. LCL. Cambridge: Harvard University Press.

Epictetus. *Discourses and Encheiridion.* 2 vols. Trans. W. A. Oldfather. LCL. Cambridge: Harvard University Press.

Epicurus: The Extant Fragments. Ed. Cyril Bailey. Oxford: Clarendon, 1926.

Eusebius. *Die Theophanie.* Ed. E. Klostermann. GCS 3/2. Leipzig: Heinrichs, 1904.

Isocrates. 3 vols. Trans. G. Norlin and L. Van Hook. LCL. Cambridge: Harvard University Press.

Jerome. *The Principal Works of St. Jerome.* Trans. W. H. Fremantle. In *Nicene and Post-Nicene Fathers of the Christian Church.* 2nd ser., vol. 6. Reprint. Grand Rapids: Eerdmans, 1968.

Joseph and Asenath. Trans. E. W. Brooks. London: SPCK, 1918.

Joseph et Aséneth. Ed. and trans. M. Philonenko. SPB. Leiden: Brill, 1968.

Josephus. 9 vols. Trans. J. St. J. Thackeray and R. Marcus et al. LCL. Cambridge: Harvard University Press.

Justin. *Die älteste Apologeten: Texte mit kurzen Einleitungen.* Ed. E. J. Goodspeed. Göttingen: Vandenhoeck & Ruprecht, 1914.

Justin. *Second Apology*. Trans. Alexander Roberts and James Donaldson. In *Ante-Nicene Fathers*, vol. 1. Reprint. Grand Rapids: Eerdmans, 1968.

Juvenal. *Satires*. Trans. G. C. Ramsey. LCL. Cambridge: Harvard University Press.

Laudatio Turiae. *Texte établi et traduit et commentaire*. Ed. and trans. Marcel Durry. Belles Lettres, 1950.

_____. *The So-Called Laudatio Turiae. Introduction, text, translation, commentary*. Ed. and trans. Erik Karl Hilding Wistrand. Studia Graeca et Latina Göteborgensia 34. Göteborg: Acta Universitatis, 1976.

Longus. *Daphnis and Chloe*. Trans. George Thornley. LCL. Cambridge: Harvard University Press.

Pseudo-Lucian. *Affairs of the Heart*. Trans. M. D. Macleod. LCL. Cambridge: Harvard University Press.

Maximus of Tyre. *Philosophumena*. Ed. Hermann Hobein. Leipzig: Teubner, 1910.

Menander. *Menandrea ex papyris et membranis vetustissimis*. Ed. Alfred Körte. Leipzig: Teubner, 1912.

_____. *The Principal Fragments*. Trans. F. G. Allinson. LCL. Cambridge: Harvard University Press.

Midrash Rabbah. 10 vols. Trans. Harry Feldman and Marcel Simon. London: Soncino, 1939.

Mishnah. Ed. and trans. Herbert Danby. Oxford: Oxford University Press, 1933.

Musonius Rufus. The Roman Socrates. Ed. and trans. C. Lutz. Yale Classical Studies 10. New Haven: Yale University Press, 1947.

Novum Testamentum Graece. 26th ed. revised. Eds. Eberhard Nestle, Erwin Nestle, Kurt Aland, and Barbara Aland. Stüttgart: Deutsche Bibelstiftung, 1979.

Ovid. *The Art of Love and Other Poems*. 2nd ed. Vol 2 of 6 vols. Trans. J. H. Mozley. LCL. Cambridge: Harvard University Press.

Pseudo-Phocylides. *Sentences of Pseudo-Phocylides*. Ed. and trans. P. W. van der Horst. SVTP 4. Leiden: Brill, 1978.

Plato. 12 vols. Trans. H. N. Fowler et al. LCL. Cambridge: Harvard University Press.

Pliny. *Letters.* 2 vols. Trans. Betty Radice. LCL. Cambridge: Harvard University Press.

Plutarch. *Moralia.* 16 vols. Trans. F. C. Babbitt et al. LCL. Cambridge: Harvard University Press.

Polybius. *Histories.* 6 vols. Trans. W. R. Paton. LCL. Cambridge: Harvard University Press.

Quintilian. *Institutio oratoria.* 4 vols. Trans. H. E. Butler. LCL. Cambridge: Harvard University Press.

Select Paryri. 5 vols. Ed. and trans. A. S. Hunt and C. C. Edgar. LCL. Cambridge: Harvard University Press.

Seneca. *Epistulae Morales.* 3 vols. Trans. R. M. Gummere. LCL. Cambridge: Harvard University Press.

Septuaginta. *Id est Vetus Testamentum graece iuxta LXX interpretes.* 6th ed. Ed. A. Rahlfs. Stüttgart: Württembergische Bibelanstalt, 1954.

Stobaeus. *Anthologium.* Ed. Thomas Gaisford. Oxford: Clarendon, 1882.

_____. *Anthologium.* 5 vols. Eds. C. Wachsmuth und O. Hense. Berlin: Weidmann, 1958.

Strabo. *Geography.* 8 vols. Trans. H. L. Jones. LCL. Cambridge: Harvard University Press.

Targum Pseudo-Jonathan ben Usiël zum Pentateuch. Ed. M. Ginsburger. Reprint. Jerusalem: Makor, 1960.

Testament of Job. Eds. and trans. Robert A. Kraft, et al. Text and Translations 5. Missoula: Scholars Press, 1974.

Testaments of the Twelve Patriarchs. A Critical Edition of the Greek Text. Ed. Marinus de Jonge. Leiden: Brill, 1978.

Tertullian. *Apology.* Trans. T. R. Glover. LCL. Cambridge: Harvard University Press.

Valerius Maximus. *Factorum et Dictorum Memorabilium Libri.* Ed. C. Kempf. Stüttgart: Teubner, 1966.

Xenophon. 7 vols. Trans. C. L. Brownson et al. LCL. Cambridge: Harvard University Press.

Xenophon of Ephesus. *Ephesiacorum.* Ed. Antonius D. Papanikolaou. Leipzig: Teubner, 1973.

COLLECTED TEXTS AND TRANSLATIONS

Arnim, H. von, ed. 1921. *Stoicorum Veterum Fragmente.* 4 vols. Leipzig: Teubner.

Charles, R. H., ed. 1913. *Apocrypha and Pseudepigrapha of the Old Testament.* 2 vols. Oxford: Clarendon.

Dessau, Hermann, ed. 1954. *Inscriptiones latinae selectae.* 3 vols in 5. Berlin: Weidmann.

Diels, Hermann, ed. and trans. 1954. *Die Fragmenta der Vorsokratiker.* 7th ed. 3 vols. Berlin: Weidmann.

Hadas, Moses, trans. 1964. *Three Greek Romances.* Indianapolis: Bobbs-Merrill.

Hercher, Rudolf, ed. 1873. *Epistolographi Graeci.* Paris: Didot.

Hennecke, Edgar and Schneemelcher, Wilhelm, eds. 1964. *New Testament Apocrypha,* vol 2. Eng. trans. ed. R. McL. Wilson. Philadelphia: Westminster.

Lipsius, Richard Adelbert. 1891. *Acta apostolorum apocrypha.* vol. 1. Leipzig: Mendelsshon.

Malherbe, Abraham J., ed. 1977a. *The Cynic Epistles: A Study Edition.* Missoula: Scholars Press.

Spengel, Leonhard, ed. 1854. *Rhetores Graeci.* 3 vols. Leipzig: Teubner.

Taylor, Thomas, trans. 1818. *Iamblichus' Life of Pythagoras, or Pythagoric Life. Accompanied by Fragments of the Ethical Writings of Certain Pythagoreans in the Doric Dialect; and a Collection of Pythagoric Sentences.* London: Valpy.

Taylor, Thomas, trans. 1822. *Political Fragments of Archytas, Charondas, Zaleucus and Other Ancient Pythagoreans Preserved by Stobaeus and also Ethical Fragments of Hierocles.* London: Whittingham.

Thesleff, Holger, ed. 1965. *The Pythagorean Texts of the Hellenistic Period.* Acta Academiae Aboensis Ser. A, Humaniora 30. Abo: Abo Akademi.

GENERAL WORKS

Allmen, Jean Jacques von. 1963. *Pauline Teaching on Marriage.* Trans. from the French. London: Faith Press.

Allo, E.-B. 1935. *Saint Paul: Première épître aux Corinthiens.* EBib. Paris: Gabalda.

Bachmann, Philipp. 1921. *Der erste Brief des Paulus an die Korinther.* Kommentar zum Neuen Testament 7. Leipzig; Erlangen: Deichert.

Balch, David L. 1972. "Backgrounds of 1 Cor. 7: Sayings of the Lord in Q; Moses as an Ascetic ΘΕΙΟΣ ΑΝΗΡ in II Cor. 3." *NTS* 18: 351-364.

_____. 1981. *Let Wives Be Submissive: The Domestic Code in 1 Peter.* SBLMS 26. Chico: Scholars Press.

_____. 1983. "1 Cor 7:32-35 and Stoic Debates about Marriage, Anxiety, and Distraction." *JBL* 102:429-439.

Balsdon, J. P. V. D. 1962. *Roman Women.* London: The Bodley Head.

_____. 1969. *Life and Leisure in Ancient Rome.* New York; St. Louis; San Francisco: McGraw-Hill.

Baltensweiler, Heinrich. 1967. *Die Ehe im Neuen Testament. Exegetische Untersuchungen über Ehe, Ehelosigkeit und Ehescheidung. ATANT.* Zürich; Stüttgart: Zwingli.

Barrett, Charles Kingsley. 1971. *The First Epistle to the Corinthians.* 2nd ed. Harper/Black New Testament Commentaries. London: Black; New York: Harper & Row.

_____. 1982. *Essays on Paul.* Philadelphia: Westminster.

Bartchy, S. Scott. 1973. *Mallon Chresai: First-Century Slavery and the Interpretation of I Corinthians 7:21.* SBL Dissertation Series, 11. Missoula: Scholars Press.

Beauvery, Robert. 1955. "σκεῦος in I Thess. 4.6a." *VD* 33:78-85.

Becker, Jürgen. 1970. *Untersuchungen zur Entstehungsgeschichte der Testamente zer zwölf Patriarchen.* AGJU 8. Leiden: Brill.

Berger, Peter L., and Luckmann, Thomas. 1966. *The Social Construction of Reality: A Treatise in the Sociology of Knowledge.* Garden City, NY: Doubleday.

Bertram, Georg. 1964. "ἔθνος, κτλ" *TDNT* 2:364-369.

Best, Ernest. 1972. *A Commentary on the First and Second Epistles to the Thessalonians.* Harper/Black New Testament Commentaries. London: Black; New York: Harper & Row.

Betz, Hans Dieter. 1979. *Galatians: A Commentary on Paul's Letter to the Churches in Galatia.* Hermeneia. Philadelphia: Fortress.

Boers, Hendrick W. 1967. "Apocalyptic Eschatology in 1 Corinthians 15." *Int* 21:50-65.

Bornkamm, Günther. 1969. "On the Understanding of Worship." In *Early Christian Experience*, trans. Paul L. Hammer. Philadelphia: Fortress. Pp. 161-180.

Boswell, John. 1980. *Christianity, Social Tolerance, and Homosexuality: Gay People in Western Europe from the Beginning of the Christian Era to the Fourteenth Century*. Chicago and London: University of Chicago Press.

Bradley, David. 1953. "The Topos as a Form in the Pauline Paraenesis." *JBL* 72:238-246.

Bruce, F. F. 1977. *Paul: Apostle of the Heart Set Free*. Grand Rapids: Eerdmans.

Campenhausen, Hans von. 1957. *Die Begründung kirchlicher Entscheidung beim Apostel Paulus*. Heidelberg: Winter.

Carcopino, Jerome. 1940. *Daily Life in Ancient Rome. The People and the City at the Height of the Empire*. New Haven: Yale University Press.

Carrington, Philip. 1940. *The Primitive Christian Catechism: A Study in the Epistles*. Cambridge: The University Press.

Chadwick, Henry. 1954. "'All Things to All Men' (I Cor. ix.22)." *NTS* I:261-275.

Collins, John J. 1983. *Between Athens and Jerusalem: Jewish Identity in the Hellenistic Diaspora*. New York: Crossroad.

Conzelmann, Hans. 1967. "Korinth und die Mädchen der Aphrodite." In *Nachrichten von der Akademie der Wissenschaften in Göttingen* 8:247-261.

_____. 1975. *1 Corinthians: A Commentary on the First Epistle to the Corinthians*. Trans. James W. Leitch. Hermeneia. Philadelphia: Fortress.

Cope, Lamar. 1978. "1 Cor 11:2-16: One Step Further." *JBL* 97:435-436.

Corbett, P. E. 1930. *The Roman Law of Marriage*. Oxford: Clarendon.

Craig, Clarence Tucker. 1951. "The First Epistle to the Corinthians: Introduction and Exegesis." In *The Interpreter's Bible*. Ed. George A. Buttrick. 12 vols. Nashville; New York: Abingdon. Vol 10, pp 1-262.

Crouch, James E. 1972. *The Origin and Intention of the Colossian Haustafel*. *FRLANT* 109. Göttingen: Vandenhoeck & Ruprecht.

Dahl, Nils Alstrup. 1967. "Paul and the Church at Corinth according to 1 Corinthians 1:10-4:21." In *Christian History and Interpretation:*

Studies Presented to John Knox, ed. William R. Farmer, C. F. D. Moule, and Richard R. Niebuhr. Cambridge: The University Press. Pp. 313-335. Now in Dahl 1977, 40-61.

_____. 1976. *Jesus in the Memory of the Early Church*. Minneapolis: Augsburg.

_____. 1977. *Studies in Paul*. Minneapolis: Augsburg.

Danker, F. W. 1972. "Under Contract: A Form-Critical Study of Linguistic Adaptation in Romans." In *Festschrift to Honor F. Wilbur Gingrich*. Ed. E. H. Barth and R. E. Cocroft. *Leiden: Brill. Pp. 91-114.*

Davies, Stevan L. 1980. *The Revolt of the Widows: The Social World of the Apocryphal Acts*. Carbondale and Edwardsville, IL: Southern Illinois University Press; London and Amsterdam: Feffer & Simons.

Delling, Gerhard. 1931. *Paulus' Stellung zu Frau und Ehe*. Stüttgart: Kohlhammer.

_____. 1959. "Eheleben," "Ehescheidung." *RAC* 4:691-719.

_____. 1968. "πλεονέκτης, κτλ." In *TDNT* 6, 266-274.

Dibelius, Martin. 1937. *An die Thessalonicher I, II; An die Philipper*. Handbuch zum Neuen Testament, 11. Tübingen: Mohr (Seibeck).

_____. 1976. *A Commentary on the Epistle of James*, revised Heinrich Greevan. Trans. Michael A. Williams. Hermeneia. Philadelphia: Fortress.

Dobschütz, Ernst von. 1909. *Die Thessalonicher-Briefe*. 7th ed. Kritisch-exegetischer Kommentar über das Neue Testament, 10. Göttingen: Vandenhoeck & Ruprecht.

Douglas, Mary. 1966. *Purity and Danger: An Analysis of Concepts of Pollution and Taboo*. London: Routledge & Kegan Paul.

_____. 1973. *Natural Symbols: Explorations in Cosmology*. 2nd ed. London: Barrie & Jenkins.

Dover, Kenneth J. 1974. *Greek Popular Morality in the Time of Plato and Aristotle*. Berkeley: University of California Press.

Dungan, David. 1971. *The Sayings of Jesus in the Churches of Paul*. Philadelphia: Fortress.

Ellicott, C. J. 1884. *A Critical and Grammatical Commentary on St. Paul's Epistles to the Thessalonians*. Andover, MA: Draper.

Elliott, J. K. 1973. "Paul's Teaching on Marriage in I Corinthians: Some Problems Reconsidered." *NTS* 19:219-225.

Enslin, Morton Scott. 1957. *The Ethics of Paul.* Nashville; New York: Abingdon.

Epstein, Louis M. 1942. *Marriage Laws in the Bible and the Talmud.* Harvard Semitic Series 12. Cambridge: Harvard University Press.

_____. 1948. *Sex Laws and Customs in Judaism.* New York: Bloch.

Fascher, Erich. 1929. "Zur Witwerschaft des Paulus und der Auslegung von I Cor 7." *ZNW* 28:62-69.

Faw, C. E. 1952. "On the Writing of First Thessalonians." *JBL* 71:217-225.

Feldman, David M. 1974. *Marital Relations Birth Control and Abortion in Jewish Law.* New York: Schocken.

Fiorenza, Elisabeth Schüssler. 1983. *In Memory of Her: A Feminist Theological Reconstruction of Christian Origins.* New York: Crossroads.

Fitzmyer, Joseph A. 1976. "The Matthean Divorce Texts and Some New Palestinian Evidence." *TS* 37:197-226.

Frame, James Everett. 1912. *A Critical and Exegetical Commentary on the Epistles of St. Paul to the Thessalonians.* ICC. Edinburgh: Clark.

Friedländer, Ludwig. 1913. *Roman Life and Manners under the Early Empire.* 2 vols. Trans. L.A. Magnus. New York: Dutton.

Funk, Robert W. 1966. *Language, Hermeneutic, and Word of God: The Problem of Language in the New Testament and Contemporary Theology.* New York: Harper & Row.

Gager, John G. 1975. *Kingdom and Community: The Social World of Early Christianity.* Englewood Cliffs, NJ: Prentice-Hall.

Gaiser, Konrad. 1974. *Für und wider die Ehe. Antike Stimmen zu einer offenen Frage.* Dialog mit der Antike 1. Munich: Heimeran.

Geytenbeek, Anton C. van. 1963. *Musonius Rufus and Greek Diatribe.* Trans. B.L. Hijmans, Jr. Rev. ed. Assen: van Gorcum.

Grant, Michael. 1975. *Eros in Pompeii: The Secret Rooms of the National Museum of Naples.* New York: Morrow.

Grosheide, F. W. 1953. *A Commentary on the First Epistle to the Corinthians.* NIC. Grand Rapids: Eerdmans.

Heinemann, Isaak. 1932. *Philons griechische und jüdische Bildung: Kultur-vergleichende Untersuchungen zu Philons Darstellung der jüdischen Gesetze.* Breslau: Marcus Verlag.

Heinrici, C. F. G. 1888. *Kritisch-Exegetisches Handbuch über den ersten Brief an die Korinther.* 7th ed. Kritisch-exegetischer Kommentar über das Neue Testament, 5. Göttingen: Vandenhoeck & Ruprecht.

Héring, Jean. 1962. *The First Epistle of Saint Paul to the Corinthians.* Trans. A. W. Heathcote and P. J. Allcock. London: Epworth.

Hock, Ronald F. 1980. *The Social Context of Paul's Ministry: Tentmaking and Apostleship.* Philadelphia: Fortress.

_____. 1982. "The Will of God and Sexual Morality: I Thessalonians 4.3-8 in its Social and Intellectual Context." An unpublished paper read to the SBL Seminar on the Thessalonian Correspondence at the annual meeting of the SBL in San Francisco, CA.

Horsley, Richard A. 1978. "'How can some of you say that there is no resurrection of the dead?' Spiritual Elitism in Corinth." *NovT* 20:203-231.

Hurd, John C. 1965. *The Origin of I Corinthians.* London: SPCK.

Jackson, C. N. 1912. "An Ancient Letter-Writer—Alciphron." In *Harvard Essays on Classical Subjects.* Ed. H. W. Smyth. Boston: Houghton Mifflin. Pp. 67-96.

Jastrow, Marcus. 1967. *A Dictionary of the Targumin, The Talmud Babli and Yerushalmi, and the Midrashic Literature.* Brooklyn: Shalom.

Jeremias, Joachim. 1926. "War Paulus Witwer?" *ZNW* 25:310-312.

_____. 1929. "Nochmals: War Paulus Witwer?" *ZNW* 28:321-323.

_____. 1953. "Zur Gedankfuhrüng in den paulinischen Briefen: (3) Die Briefzitate in I. Kor 8, 1-13." In *Studia Paulina in Honorem Johannis de Zwann Septuagenarii.* Ed. J.N. Sevenster and W.C. van Unnik. Haarlem: Bohn. Pp. 151-153. Now in Jeremias 1966, 269-273.

_____. 1966. *Abba.* Göttingen: Vandenhoeck & Ruprecht.

Jewett, Robert. 1971. *Paul's Anthropological Terms.* Leiden: Brill.

Johns, Catherine. 1982. *Sex or Symbol: Erotic Images of Greece and Rome.* Austin: Unversity of Texas Press.

Jonge, Marinus de. 1975. *Studies on the Testaments of the Twelve Patriarchs. Text and Interpretation.* STVP 3. Leiden: Brill.

Kähler, Else. 1960. *Die Frau in den paulinischen Briefen. Unter Berücksichtigung des Begriffes Unterordnung.* Zürich: Gotthelf.

Käsemann, Ernst. 1960. "Die Anfänge christlicher Theologie." *ZTK* 57:162-185. Now in Käsemann 1969, 82-107.

_____. 1962. "Zum Thema der urchristlichen Apokalyptik." *ZTK* 59:257-284. Now in Käsemann 1969, 108-138.

_____. 1969. *New Testament Questions of Today.* Trans. W. J. Montague. London: SCM; Philadelphia: Fortress.

Keck, Leander E. 1974. "On the Ethos of Early Christians." *JAAR* 42:435-452.

Klassen, William. 1978. "Foundations for Pauline Sexual Ethics as seen in I Thess. 4.1-8." In *SBL Seminar Papers.* Ed. Paul Achtemeier. Missoula: Scholars Press. Vol 2, pp. 159-181.

Koester, Helmut. 1961. Review of Ulrich Wilckens, *Weisheit und Torheit. Gnomon* 33:590-595.

Kümmel, Werner Georg. 1975. *Introduction to the New Testament.* Trans. Howard C. Kee. Nashville and New York: Abingdon.

_____. 1954. "Verlobung und Heirat bei Paulus (I. Cor 7, 36-38)." In *Neutestamentliche Studien für Rudolf Bultmann.* BZNW 21. Berlin: Töpelmann. 275-295.

Kürzinger, Josef. 1978. "Frau und Mann nach I Kor 11.11f." *BZ* 22:270-275.

Lesky, Albin. 1966. *A History of Greek Literature.* Trans. James Willis and Cornelis de Heer. New York: Crowell.

Lewis, Naphtali and Reinhold, Meyer. 1955. *Roman Civilization.* Vol 2: *The Empire.* New York: Columbia University Press.

Liddell, Henry George and Scott, Robert. 1968. *A Greek-English Lexicon.* Rev. ed. Henry Stuart Jones. Oxford: Clarendon.

Lietzmann, Hans and Kümmel, Werner Georg. 1949. *An die Korinther.* 4th ed. HNT 9. Tübingen: Mohr [Siebeck].

Lightfoot, Joseph Barber. 1895. *Notes on the Epistles of St. Paul.* Ed. posthumously by J. Rendel Harris. London: Macmillan.

Lösch, Stefan. 1947. "Christliche Frauen in Corinth." *TQ* 127:216-261.

MacMullen, Ramsey. 1974. *Roman Social Relations.* New Haven and London: Yale University Press.

Malherbe, Abraham J. 1968. "The Beasts at Ephesus." *JBL* 87:71-80.

_____. 1970. "'Gentle as a Nurse': The Cynic Background of 1 Thess ii." *NovT* 12:203-217.

_____. 1977b. *Social Aspects of Early Christianity*. Baton Rouge; London: Louisiana State University Press.

_____. 1982. "Self-Definition among Epicureans and Cynics." In *Jewish and Christian Self-Definition*. Ed. Ben F. Meyer and E.P. Sanders. Philadelphia: Fortress. Vol. 3, pp. 46-59.

_____. 1983a. "Exhortation in First Thessalonians." *NovT* 25:238-256.

_____. 1983b. *Social Aspects of Early Christianity*. 2nd ed., enlarged. Philadelphia: Fortress.

_____. forthcoming. "Hellenistic Moralists and the New Testament." *ANRW*, pt. 2, vol 26.

Manning, C. E. 1973. "Seneca and the Stoics on the Equality of the Sexes." *Mnemosyne* 26:170-177.

Maurer, Christian. 1971. "σκεῦος" In *TDNT* 7:358-367.

Meeks, Wayne A. 1974. "The Image of the Androgyne: Some Uses of a Symbol in Earliest Christianity." *HR* 13:165-208.

_____. 1975. "The Social World of Early Christianity." *BCSR* 6:1,4-5.

_____. 1979. "'Since then you would need to go out of the world': Group Boundaries in Pauline Christianity." In *Critical History and Biblical Faith: New Testament Perspectives*. Ed. T.J. Ryan. Villanova: College Theology Society, 1979.

_____. 1983. *First Urban Christians. The Social World of the Apostle Paul*. New Haven and London: Yale University Press.

Meyer, Heinrich August Wilhelm. 1881. *Critical and Exegetical Handbook to the Epistles to the Corinthians*. Trans. D.D. Bannerman and D. Hunter. Edinburgh: Clark.

Milligan, George. 1908. *St. Paul's Epistles to the Thessalonians*. London: Macmillan.

Moffatt, James. 1938. *The First Epistle of Paul to the Corinthians*. Moffatt New Testament Commentary. London: Hodder and Stoughton.

Moore, George Foot. 1927. *Judaism in the First Centuries of the Christian Age*. 3 vols. Cambridge: Harvard University Press.

Morris, Leon. 1958. *The First Epistle of Paul to the Corinthians*. London: Tyndale.

Moulton, James Hope and Milligan, George. 1930. *The Vocabulary of the Greek New Testament: Illustrated from the Papyri and Other Non-Literary Sources*. Grand Rapids: Eerdmans.

Mullins, Terence Y. 1980. "Topos as a NT Form." *JBL* 99:541-547.

Murphy-O'Connor, Jerome. 1976. "The Non-Pauline Character of 1 Corinthians 11:2-16?" *JBL* 95:615-621.

_____. 1980. "Sex and Logic in 1 Corinthians 11:2-16." *CBQ* 42:482-500.

_____. 1981. "The Divorced Woman in 1 Cor 7:10-11." *JBL* 100:601-606.

Nickelsburg, G. W. 1981. *Jewish Literature Between the Bible and Mishnah: A Historical and Literary Intriduction*. Philadelphia: Fortress.

Nock, Arthur Darby. 1933. *Conversion*. Oxford: Clarendon.

Noth, Martin. 1965. *Leviticus*. Old Testament Library. Philadelphia: Fortress.

Oepke, Albrecht. 1959. "Ehe I." *RAC* 4:650-666.

Pagels, Elaine H. 1974. "Paul and Women: A Reponse to Recent Discussion." *JAAR* 42:538-549.

Pax, Elpidius. 1971. "Beobachtungen zur Konvertitensprache im ersten Thessalonicherbrief." *Studii Biblici Franciscani Analecta* 21:220-261.

_____. 1972. "Konvertitenprobleme im ersten Thessalonicherbrief." *Bibleb* 13:24-37.

Pomeroy, Sarah B. 1975. *Goddesses, Whores, Wives, and Slaves: Women in Classical Antiquity*. New York: Schocken.

Praechter, Karl. 1901. *Hierocles der Stoiker*. Leipzig: Weicher.

Preisker, Herbert. 1927. *Christentum und Ehe in ersten drei Jahrhunderten: Eine Studie zur Kulturgeschichte der alten Welt*. Berlin: Trowitzsch & Sohn.

Rigaux, Béda. 1956. *Saint Paul: Les Épîtres aux Thessaloniciens*. Ebib. Paris: Gabalda.

Robertson, Archibald and Plummer, Alfred. 1914. *A Critical and Exegetical Commentary on the First Epistle of St. Paul to the Corinthians*. 2nd ed. Edinburgh: Clark.

Rohde, Erwin. 1914. *Der griechische Roman*. 3rd ed. Leipzig: Breitkopf und Härtel.

Safrai, Samuel. 1976. "Home and Family." In *The Jewish People in the First Century*. Ed. S. Safrai and M. Stern. Philadelphia: Fortress. Vol 2, pp 728-792.

Sampley, J. Paul. 1980. *Pauline Partnership in Christ: Christian Community and Commitment in Light of Roman Law*. Philadelphia: Fortress.

Sanders, H.A. 1938. "A Latin Marriage Contract." *TAPA* 69:104-116.

Schweizer, Eduard. 1979. "Traditional ethical patterns in the Pauline and post-Pauline letters and their development (lists of vices and housetables)." In *Text and Interpretation: Studies in the New Testament presented to Matthew Black*. Eds. Ernest Best and R. McL. Wilson. Cambridge: The University Press. Pp. 195-209.

Scroggs, Robin. 1972. "Paul and the Eschatological Woman." In *JAAR* 40:215-303.

_____. 1974. "Paul and the Eschatological Woman: Revisited." In *JAAR* 42:523-527.

_____. 1983. *The New Testament and Homosexuality*. Philadelphia: Fortress.

Segal, Moses H. 1958. ספר בן סירה (The Book of Ben Sira). Hebrew Text, with commentary. Jerusalem: Bailik Institute.

Selwyn, Edward Gordon. 1958. *The First Epistle of St. Peter*. 2nd ed. London: Macmillan.

Smith, Jonathan Z. 1975. "The Social Description of Early Christianity." In *RSR* 1:19-25.

Stadele, Alfons. 1980. *Die Briefe des Pythagoras und der Pythagoreer*. Beiträge zur klassischen Philologie 115. Maisenheim am Glan: Hain.

Theissen, Gerd. 1974a. "Soziale Integration und sakramentales Handeln: Eine Analyse von 1 Cor XI 17-34." *NovT* 24:179-205. Now in Theissen 1982, 145-174.

_____. 1974b. "Soziale Schichtung in der korinthischen Gemeinde." *ZNW* 65:232-272. Now in Theissen 1982, 69-120.

_____. 1975a. "Die soziologische Auswertung religiöser Überlieferungen." *Kairos* 17:248-299.

_____. 1975b. "Die Starken und Schwachen in Korinth: Soziologische Analyse eines theologischen Streites." *EvT* 35:155-172. Now in Theissen 1982, 121-144.

_____. 1982. *The Social Setting of Pauline Christianity: Essays on Corinth*. Ed. and trans. John H. Schütz. Philadelphia: Fortress.

Thesleff, Holger. 1961. *An Introduction to the Pythagorean Writings of the Hellenistic Period*. Acta Academiae Aboenisis, Humaniora 24.3. Abo: Abo Akademi.

Thiselton, A. C. 1977. "Realized Eschatology at Corinth." *NTS* 24:510-526.

Thraede, Kurt. 1977. "Ärger mit der Freiheit. Die Bedeutung von Frauen in Theorie und Praxis der alten Kirche." In *Freunde in Christus werden . . ." Die Beziehung von Mann und Frau als Frage an Theologie und Kirche*. Ed. G. Scharffenorth. Gelnhausen; Berlin: Burckhardthaus. Pp. 35-182.

Thurian, Max. [1959]. *Marriage and Celibacy*. Trans. Norma Emerton. With an introduction by Roger Schutz. London: SCM.

Trompf, G. W. 1980. "On Attitudes Toward Women in Paul and Paulinist Literature 1 Corinthians 11:3-16 and its Context." *CBQ* 42:196-215.

Unnik, W. C. van. 1960. "Die Rücksicht auf die Reaktion der Nicht-Christen als Motiv in der altchristlichen Paränese." In *Judentum, Urchristentum, Kirche: Festschrift für Walther Eltester*. Berlin: Töpelmann. Pp. 221-234.

VanderKam, J. C. 1977. *Textual and Historical Studies in the Book of Jubilees*. HSM 14. Missoula: Scholars Press.

Walker, William O. 1975. "1 Corinthians 11:2-16 and Paul's Views Regarding Women." In *JBL* 94:94-110.

_____. 1983. "The 'Theology of Woman's Place' and the 'Paulinist' Tradition." *Semeia* 28:101-112.

Webster, T. B. L. 1960. *Studies in Menander*. Manchester: Manchester University Press.

Weiss, Johannes. 1910. *Der erste Korintherbrief*. 9th ed. Kritisch-exegetischer Kommentar über das Neue Testament, 5. Göttingen: Vandenhoeck & Ruprecht.

Wendland, Heinz-Dietrich. 1962. *Die Briefe an die Korinther*. NTD 7. 8th ed. Göttingen: Vandenhoeck & Ruprecht.

Wendland, Paul. 1895. "Philo und die kynisch-stoische Diatribe." In *Beitrage zur geschichte der griechischen Philosophie und Religion: Fest.* Hermann Diels. Ed. Paul Wendland and Otto Kern. Berlin: Georg Reimer.

Whitten, J. 1982. "A Neglected Meaning for *SKEUOS* in I Thess. 4.4." *NTS* 28:142-143.

Wilckens, Ulrich. 1959. *Weisheit und Torheit.* BHT 26. Tübingen: Mohr [Siebeck].

Wilson, Jack H. 1968. "The Corinthians Who Say There Is No Resurrection of the Dead." *ZNW* 59:90-117.

Wolbert, Werner. 1981. *Ethische Argumentation und Paränese in 1 Kor 7.* Düsseldorf: Patmos.

Wolff, H. J. 1939. *Written and Unwritten Marriages in Hellenistic and Post-Classical Roman Law.* Philological Monographs 9. Lancaster PA: Lancaster.

INDEX

BIBLICAL REFERENCES

Old Testament and Apocrypha

New Testament

ANCIENT SOURCES

I. Jewish

II. Christian

III. Classical

IV. Inscriptions and Papyri